HIDDEN
HITCHCOCK

T0385558

HIDDEN HITCHCOCK

D. A. Miller

The University of Chicago Press | *Chicago and London*

The University of Chicago Press, Chicago 60637
The University of Chicago Press, Ltd., London
© 2016 by The University of Chicago
All rights reserved. Published 2016.
Paperback edition 2017
Printed in the United States of America

23 22 21 20 19 18 17   2 3 4 5 6

ISBN-13: 978-0-226-37467-3 (cloth)
ISBN-13: 978-0-226-51434-5 (paper)
ISBN-13: 978-0-226-37470-3 (e-book)
DOI: 10.7208/chicago/9780226374703.001.0001

Library of Congress Cataloging-in-Publication Data

Names: Miller, D. A., 1948– author.
Title: Hidden Hitchcock / D. A. Miller.
Description: Chicago ; London : The University of Chicago Press, 2016. |
    Includes bibliographical references.
Identifiers: LCCN 2015046038 | ISBN 9780226374673 (cloth : alk. paper) |
    ISBN 9780226374703 (e-book)
Subjects: LCSH: Hitchcock, Alfred, 1899–1980. | Motion pictures.
Classification: LCC PN1998.3.H58 M55 2016 | DDC 791.4302/33092—dc23
    LC record available at http://lccn.loc.gov/2015046038

♾ This paper meets the requirements of ANSI/NISO Z39.48-1992
(Permanence of Paper).

It's as if I had one extra sense, one more than the others have, but not completely developed, a sense that's there and makes itself noticed, but doesn't function.

Musil

Contents

Preview

Even a work of criticism may be in danger of spoilers; sometimes, the less you know from the trailer, the better. And so
I refrain here from offering a comprehensive summary that
might eliminate any apparent need to read beyond it. Instead
I present a short dossier of the key conceptions, forms, devices, and materials that will be set to work (harmoniously
or not) in the essays to follow.

Public Style, Secret Style

Behind the impersonal detachment of a sovereign stylist,
there often stands a damaged or disparaged person. Hitchcock is a famous—and self-conscious—case in point. The
homely fat man who "appears" onscreen only to decamp
straightaway, as if he knew he were hopelessly out of place
amongst cinema's beautiful people, is also the magisterial
Auteur whose invisible hand has put these people in place—
and will be bringing some of them, qua characters, to places
they would never choose to be. The Hitchcock cameo always

implies, along with his social abjection, the sado-artistic revenge he is taking for it from the pinnacle of cinematic mastery. And yet for all that, Hitchcock's antisocial malice must generally strike us as pretty mild, even jovial. Though the man shows himself hastily retreating from the social field, its demands and norms remain in force to determine the substance and style of the work. Typically, the plots devised by this onscreen loner dramatize the most basic social obligation: that formation of the Couple for which murder and mayhem are merely especially thrilling catalysts. And no film style has more successfully courted mass-audience understanding and approval than Hitchcock's. In his supremely lucid narrative communication, nothing deserves our attention that his camera doesn't go out of its way to point out. This cinema has plenty of ploys, but none it doesn't let us see through; suspense, the chief of these, depends precisely on forewarning us in such a way that our pleasure, if seldom unmixed with fear, is never spoiled by confusion. With a super-accessible style working hard to rehearse the emergence of the very unit of social organization, could there be (say at least until *Psycho* [1960] and *The Birds* [1963]) a more sociable author than Hitchcock?

I have been describing Hitchcock's *manifest* style, his style reduced to its universally intelligible and beloved codes. But as anyone who has seen a Hitchcock film knows, the director primes us to be considerably more alert than his spoon-feeding requires. In addition to our instrumental attention, we find ourselves possessed of a watchfulness that seems to have no object or use. Even when Hitchcock is not enjoining us to "pay attention," we remain poised behind a pane of vigilance, as if expecting to see something besides his unmissable danger signals and loud significance alerts. But it appears we never do. Our vigilance stays on idle, never sufficiently roused to put undesignated objects under the focused scrutiny we obediently bestow on the designated ones. A strangely futile vigilance, it irritates our vision only by virtue of being palpably in excess of what we are being *asked* to see; ready to be as observant as Sherlock Holmes, we are challenged with only the most elementary cases. Inevitably, we can't help sensing that there is more to meet the eye in Hitchcock than, in his viewer-friendly manner, he arranges to *greet* the eye. To put the point bluntly, everything we *are* asked to see in Hitchcock feels a bit disappointing: a facade that blocks our view of all that we imagine we *might* see in the visual field. To watch a Hitchcock film is thus always to come under the spell of a *hidden* Hitchcock, and to want, somehow, to focus our attention on this imaginary thing or being. Whence the paradox of Hitchcock's cultural reception. On the one hand, he is widely regarded as having little to say (a pure entertainer who toils in the "empty" thriller genre); on the other, his stand-out style is the object of an enormous fascination that those who feel it hardly know how to explain.

This excess attention no doubt accounts for the pronounced tendency of Hitchcock criticism to "close-read" his films. Even before the home-system revolution democratized the practice, critics like Raymond Bellour and William Rothman worked from prints that they would dissect shot by shot and sometimes virtually frame by frame. With their editing table or Lafayette analyzer, these great close viewers did what most of us only dreamed of doing—until the day when, with that thaumaturgic genie successively known as a Betamax, VHS, or DVD player at our command, we could attempt it ourselves. And yet, by and large, even such close viewing remains in thrall to the primacy of a film's narrative structure;

this is true even of an auteurist critic like Rothman, who allegorically reconfigures the given story as "the author's story."[1] As a consequence, what close viewing finds under its microscope tends to accord with our unassisted observations when watching the film under theatrical conditions. Though close viewing often brings out things we hadn't noticed, it typically uses them to explicate and enhance the things we had. It validates our normal narrative-driven viewing by extending its range, deepening its implications, and generally producing ever subtler proofs of its coherence.[2] You might say that it "repays attention" in a double sense. Not only is it demonstrably worth everyone's time and effort; it also seconds the priorities of our naïve first attention. In its own sometimes abstruse way, it piggy-backs on the social uptake of Hitchcock's public style.

It is my project here to trace a different, more devious route taken by the surplus scrutiny that Hitchcock mobilizes in us. In contrast to the games that he is known to play with his Pavlovianly trained mass audience,[3] I postulate a game he would be playing with that absurdly, pointlessly watchful spectator who dwells within us all, but whom, as members of a mass audience, or as critics in loyal alignment with it, we mostly put on lockdown; and whom I call the *Too*-Close Viewer.[4] In this game, and for this viewer alone, Hitchcock would cultivate, alongside his manifest style with its hyperlegible images, a secret style that sows these images with radical duplicity. The type of duplicity to which this book gives emblematic pride of place is the hidden picture, in which a strongly narrativized image has been fashioned to conceal something that—if ever seen—would not enhance its coherence, but explode it. Imagine a small continuity error made on purpose, or a Hitchcock cameo fashioned so as *not* to be seen, or a narrative image secretly doubling for a figure of speech in the manner of a charade, and you will have anticipated three key subtypes of Hitchcock's hidden picturing. I take all such hidden pictures as sporadic but insistent marks of a perverse counternarrative in Hitchcock that for no reason—or for no *good enough* reason—takes the viewer out of the story and out of the social compact its telling presupposes. Into what is hard to say. Structurally, the hidden pictures resist being integrated into the narrative or any ostensible intentionality; and whatever we might say about any one of them as a species of *content* falls markedly short of accounting for their enigma as a recurring *form* of Hitchcock's film-writing. It is as though, at the heart of the manifest style, there pulsed an irregular extra beat, the surreptitious "murmur" of its undoing that only the Too-Close Viewer could apprehend.

The Hidden Picture Game

How does the game work? Let me demonstrate its paradigm with a passage from an early Hitchcock film I won't be discussing later. In *Murder!* (1930), the foreman of the jury that tries Diana Baring is impatient for a conviction. He cuts off initial discussion with an appeal to the obviousness of sums: "The best thing for us all to do is to write down our opinions on a piece of paper, and then we can see how we stand." From behind the foreman's shoulder, we watch him write his own ballot, then receive, read, and sort the others. In a continuous shot that lasts over half a minute, the camera neither cuts nor moves; we see the process in its entirety and with the utmost clarity, as if the filming were meant to match the count in sheer straightforwardness (19:11–19:54). For the foreman, however, the sorting proves unexpectedly laborious, and for the spectator, curiously tense. The first and second ballots, guilty and not-guilty respectively, efficiently set up the two opposing piles. The foreman starts to put the third ballot, a vote for guilty, in the not-guilty pile, catches himself, and resumes sorting. But the blunder he has almost made once, he almost makes twice again: not only does he put a second guilty vote in the not-guilty pile, he also proceeds to put a not-guilty vote in the guilty pile. Having rectified these mistakes, too, he counts the at last properly sorted ballots and announces the result: "That makes seven guilty and three not guilty. There are two not in." The jury's subsequent deliberation confirms his numbers: two jurors have not voted, and three have voted not-guilty. All five will speedily be persuaded, not to say bullied, into the duodecimal unanimity of a death sentence. The foreman has got what he wanted; and his achievement has been as easy—and almost the same thing—as counting to ten.

We had, of course, expected this outcome, and not just on account of the foreman's pushy leadership; that leadership, rather, bespoke the structural law of the romantic whodunit, which requires Diana to be innocent but to be found guilty; were it otherwise, so early in the film, there would be no place for the plot to go, no point at which Sir John, the thespian turned detective, could "enter," resolve the mystery, and woo Diana in the bargain. In this sense, the sorting shot falls appreciably flat; it might almost be singled out as a bad example of the thing Hitchcock is so good at: suspense. Though possessing all the hyperannotation proper to suspense (one ballot, then another, and another), it never generates sufficiently high stakes. We cannot possibly imagine that Diana will be hanged because of a sorting error that would surely be caught before it became fatal. And yet despite this failure, the shot remains vaguely gripping, as though we were in fact waiting for something—something other than the verdict— and also waiting to identify it. For no obvious reason, we remain on the lookout.

As a Too-Close Viewer whose powers of observation are in equal measure excited and frustrated by all this, I too wait. I watch closely—too closely, in all likelihood, for anything to come of it. But as it happens, something does—something breaks through the pane. For despite the narrative's contention that the foreman has counted exactly ten ballots, this information is flatly contradicted by the image onscreen. I have only to look—and hasn't the shot done everything possible to afford a plain view?—in order to count, not ten ballots, but eleven, and not seven guilty votes, but eight. Given the confirmed counts of abstentions and not-guilty ballots, this twelve-person jury has somehow, nonsensically, cast thirteen votes for Diana's conviction! In the extra ballot, I recognize the deliberate double-dealing of the scene. The business of properly sorting the ballots was a monte-like ruse to prevent us from ever counting them; the game we thought we were playing with Hitchcock screened a trick he was playing on us. I have stumbled upon a hidden picture, without quite knowing it was there to be found. Though this picture demonstrably exists, the narrative does not—and cannot—acknowledge it; on the contrary, it is the narrative, with its ostensible sorting drama, that has kept the extra guilty ballot, entirely visible, from actually being seen.

But the burden of excess attention, which one might think had been blessedly lifted from my shoulders by this discovery, persists in the form of two new, more pressing difficulties. The first is that, however indisputable my finding, I don't know quite what to make of it. The extra ballot seems to have no clear hermeneutic destiny, and when I try to give it one, I catch myself stretching. It is not that there is *nothing* to say about it, only that, in the community of Hitchcock spectators with their shared understandings and consolidating narratives, there isn't *enough* to give it traction anywhere but on a list of film trivia. I have just mentioned, for instance, that the extra ballot brings the final tally of votes to an unlucky 13, but the point seems as silly as it is true. In a film that begins with the image of a church clock set to one thirty, why bother to *conceal* this banal signifier of the ominousness that is Hitchcock's stock-in-trade? And though it is also quite plausible to regard the ballot as the metacinematic sign of an Author whose hand seems almost literally at work in shaping the narrative as he pleases, this does not explain why such a sign is produced as a hidden picture in which either one follows the narrative, and fails to see this hand, or one perceives the hand, and lets the narrative collapse into absurdity.

No, the force of the hidden picture does not lie in whatever glib meanings its *content* may be hosting, but in its *form* as an enactment—latent if you don't see it, overwhelming if you do—of a semiotic stoppage productive only of nonsense. Even considered (as it can hardly not be) as a sign of Hitchcock himself, the hidden ballot is an all but unreadable index of a very uncommunicative Hitchcock. Instead of the cameo's essentially comic guarantee of a "Hitchcock movie" as we know it, this Hitchcock would figure a radically private, singular, and inassimilable Author who, paradoxically, may only emerge on the sudden death of the sociable narrative style for which he is known. Prevailing only at the expense of his work, Hitchcock's person has nothing personable about it here; it has shrunk down to the signature of sheer intractability.

My second new burden follows on the first one. Ten to one I am the only person to have noticed the hidden picture, which has gone unremarked even in so painstakingly detailed an account of *Murder!* as Rothman's.[5] Given my inability to say much about it, I fear that the very act of observing this uncounted and unaccounted-for oddity turns me into a sort of oddball, too. As the sighter of the unimportant, and indeed the anti-important, I find myself overwhelmed not by the heady elation of Cortez, but by disagreeable feelings of solitude and isolation: close to Hitchcock, if you will, but to a Hitchcock with whom I had never imagined, let alone desired, this kind of intimacy. The accident of my observation—which I seemed to fall into like a trap—has caused me to drop out of the universality of Hitchcockian spectatorship, and I can't talk my way back into it. "Am I the only one?" The hoary question suddenly feels apt again.

My new problems are eminently social ones, as though, by means of all these relays, Hitchcock's primordial out-of-placeness had come cunningly to roost as my own. Both what I find and my act of finding it make me as eccentric as the inconsequential hidden picture I have brought out of the woodwork. Before I fell into the game, my supererogatory vigilance had been like other spectators'—a diffuse, unspecified potential that had merely colored our Hitchcock-watching mood in varying degrees of intensity. But now I have actually found something—something radically discordant with the film we have all been watching, and belonging to another film that I may be the only one to see. *Our* vague, indeterminate watchfulness has crystallized into *my* act of spotting an intentionally hidden object. By a cruel dialectic, the original objectlessness has become the triviality of this object, just as the original universality now gets expressed as the social marginality of its observer. This is the dialectic that Hitchcock's Too-Close Viewer, if he is to state his case at all, is fated to live with. That case entails publicizing not just the idiosyncrasy of his findings, but also, more radically, the idiosyncrasy of his critical practice as it simultaneously over-reads and underinterprets these findings, presenting them in extensive detail, while failing to wrap them in adequate—socializable—importance.

I/He

Hitchcock's game only exists insofar as it finds a partner whom it causes to feel intensely singular; it is only half described unless the objective fact of the hidden pictures is yoked to the subjective experience of the game's implicit support. One must look closely not only at Hitchcock, but also at oneself looking. Hence, as you've just seen, I adopt the expedient of giving this work a Narrator, a speaker who is the game's critical exegete only insofar as he is also, more clamorously, the game's disadvantaged other player. He is born as a grammatical and generic swerve from the first-person plural of critical commentary to the first-person singular of an extraordinary tale. For his experience is fundamentally fantastical, blurring the boundaries between subject and object, chance and design, and, most pertinently, between the inside and outside of cinema's fourth wall. As he submits to the various mental states of surprise, suspense, suspicion, discovery, dizziness, disappointment, isolation, and folly entailed in looking at Hitchcock too closely, his ubiquitously rummaging eyes seem to turn watching a Hitchcock film into the experience of being *in* one.

You would be perfectly right to read this Narrator as a construct of myself. But given that he speaks of nothing but his fanatic observation of certain Hitchcock films, he is hardly the Rousseauistic autobiographer bent on confessing all. And since he does everything in his power to convince you that what he observes is objectively present in the image, as part of its deliberate structuration, neither can he quite be the Barthesian phenomenologist of *Camera Lucida*, whose wrenching experience of certain visual details—the punctums— draws him not to the verifiable aesthetic of the photographer, but deep into the private space of the unique being who scans them. Barthes remains perfectly consistent in refusing even to show us the photograph that touches him most profoundly: "It exists only for me." By contrast, my Narrator, far from forbidding you to see Hitchcock's concealments-in-plain-sight, defies you to continue overlooking them. This Narrator is myself, then, merely to the extent that I have surrendered my person (temperament, imagery, history, habits, moods, memories, taste, style, whatever seemed required) to the task of fashioning him as—and only as—a Too-Close Viewer.

As you have also already seen, I sometimes refer to the Too-Close Viewer in the masculine third-person singular. Who, what, is this "he"? Not, certainly, the obsolete form of today's all-inclusive "he or she"; the definitionally singular Too-Close Viewer can afford no such pretension to speak for everyone: universality would abolish him! Even less does "he" mean to restrict the potential for too-close viewing to one gender. The pronoun does affirm, though, that, when anyone realizes this potential, he or she will necessarily have to tell—and theorize—the story of a specific individual.

"He," then, is still representing the "I" who is the Too-Close Viewer, but this time by anticipating the social destiny prepared for his eccentricity as such: that of a minor character.

Anachronisms

It is not that you *couldn't* count the jurors' ballots during a theatrical viewing of *Murder!* But you would be unlikely to do so; and had the idea occurred to you, you would find it preposterously inconvenient to verify your result. Obviously, to examine the sorting shot repeatedly and in detail, I made use of a DVD player. You might say that the ability of the latter to interrupt continuity gave me more control over the image, but you might equally say that its capacity for randomizing attention gave the image a greater power to impose itself on me. In either case, my very perception of the extra ballot must be regarded as an anachronism, the artifact of a latter-day technology with the power to circumvent the twinned sine qua nons of classic cinema in the movie-house: the irresistible movement of images and the irreversible momentum of the story. Even as an anachronism, of course, it may be a useful tool, somewhat in the way that a computer program helps us determine a writer's linguistic habits; Laura Mulvey: "The fragmentation of narrative continuity may also be the discovery of a pattern that has been clouded by identification, action, or suspense."[6] And in dealing with a hidden picture, this anachronism can hardly be thought irrelevant, much less inimical, to artistic intention. Both as concept and structure, the hidden picture necessitates ruses of concealment that can never *not* be intentional; by definition, this is a picture designed to be *invisible at first glance*. In the medium of classic cinema, whose typical products have been conceived for consumption at a single theatrical viewing, the hidden picture is an acutely contradictory structure, at loggerheads with the immediately sociable readerliness of traditional filmmaking in general and with Hitchcock's manifest style in particular. Different in this from the well-known children's game, Hitchcock's hidden pictures imply the outrageous proposition that you need to see a film more than once without even knowing if, how, or why you need to.

It is not, then, just a certain kind of viewer who dreamed of some magical means by which he might put Hitchcock's images under the closer scrutiny that, even at first sight, he felt they deserved. Hitchcock too seems to have anticipated, like Rose in *The Wrong Man* (1956), that "something like this would happen." But he also surely knew that the capsules in which he buried his hidden pictures would not be opened, if ever, for a long while. As Hitchcock's Too-Close Viewer, I owe my existence at least as much to the enigmatic *withholding* that characterizes his secret style as I do to the technology that allows me a sometimes remunerative—and sometimes merely frustrating—closer look at it. The anachronism of my viewing practice draws out—and indeed has been drawn out by—the *untimeliness* of Hitchcock's filmmaking method in contriving effects whose perception it postpones to a maturity date no one may live to see. So little have we come to terms with the essential perverseness of this method that, though Hitchcock is the most written-about director in film history, and for all the exasperation and loneliness I have just been expressing, it remains my serene operating assumption that we have barely begun to look at his work!

And yet, given that the technological basis of too-close viewing appears to be doomed, how much time is left to do this? My practice is not only anachronistic with respect to the old norms of theatrical viewing; it is also on the verge of becoming superannuated vis-à-vis new norms born from streaming. If the digital disc was the Hitchcockophile's dream come true, the same can hardly be said of the *streamed text*; difficult or even impossible to rewind, fast-forward, slow, and step, it reproduces all the frustrations of theatrical viewing, while retaining none of its virtues (nothing less like cinematic flow than buffering!). The New Atlantis may be, like the old, sinking out of view; I work while I have light.

Continuity Riddles and Understyle

In *Vertigo* (1958), just as Scottie's DeSoto starts tailing Madeleine's Jaguar down a San Francisco alley, I see a crew member's hand flag a piece of film equipment; and at the end of the same film, I see the shadow of a camera flit in retreat across the mission campanile. I observe a boom mike toggling between Roger and Eve at Union Station in *North by Northwest* (1959), another dropping down a wall of the police station in *The Wrong Man*. And it goes without saying that I do not miss the lens flare that accompanies the swinging light bulb during the climax of *Psycho*! What's more, from one shot to the next, my eyes behold a veritable wonderland in which a figurine that no one can have touched shifts position; a parked car that no one has had time to move changes color and model; ice cubes melt as unnaturally fast as the sun goes down; and the very walls are abruptly razed, re-erected, razed again. The Too-Close Viewer detects countless such violations of classical filmmaking's supposed rules; his lot is not a happy one.

These continuity violations present a different kind of duplicity from the hidden pictures. A hidden picture is a figure deliberately concealed in plain view; once I identify one, it is impossible to doubt the premeditation behind it. By contrast, the continuity violation invariably causes me to ask, "Did Hitchcock intend it?" Sometimes, I think, the violation must be a simple mistake; could anything but inadvertence be responsible for the Oz-like car of a different color? At other times, I am convinced that the violation is the product of art, a thing Hitchcock has overseen rather than overlooked. *Psycho*'s lens flare, to take this uniquely well-documented instance, purposely invites us to metacinematic reflection; it is a sort of cameo of the apparatus. And an obvious artistic liberty dictates the shifting of the Oriental figurine in *Dial M for Murder* (1954) so that it reinforces the image's dramatic as well as compositional center: it is "looking" just where *we* should look. But most of the time, I am not sure: my certainty as to Hitchcock's intention or lack thereof is as rare as corroborating records. What is certain, though, is that, having perceived these violations, I can never unsee them. I can never mentally excise them from the visual field in the interest of a coherent narrative image. Their visual insistence thus fuses with their semantic ambiguity to create little irresolvable cruxes all over Hitchcock's cinema.

Barthes once observed that mass-culture myth "essentially aims at causing an immediate impression—it does not matter if one is later allowed to see through the myth, its action is assumed to be stronger than the rational explanations which may later belie it."[7] However little else they share with Barthesian myth, the continuity errors in Hitchcock strike me in a similar way; rational explanations (always belated, usually uncertain) never explain them away. Hence, in following the strong narrative drive of a Hitchcock film, I am also compelled to register its counterpropulsion to entropy: clean lines blur, and chaos stirs up the narrative sediment. On top of that, I can't stop myself from bringing even the most probable errors into formal and thematic relations with other elements in the visual field that are patently planned. Before I know it, concatenations have been forged and surmises set afloat, as by a detective theorizing in advance of the facts. Even when I choose to abandon my conjectures as false, or suspend them as undecidable, they remain the background—I might almost say, the very ground—of my understanding.

No doubt, the visual cacophony I find in Hitchcock is latent in all narrative films, just as my experience of this cacophony is simply the "outed" version of normal perception. But if continuity errors are hardly unique to Hitchcock, his do acquire an uncommon hold on us when noticed. It might appear that this hold owes mainly to their shock value as instances of Error within the legend of Perfection. Little rebellions of filmmaking contingencies against Hitchcock's mastery, they would counter the widespread assumption that this godlike director can do no wrong. And yet who has a more exuberant imagination of error than the perfectionist—and whose task, thanks to this imagination, is more Sisyphean? Far more interesting than the obvious resistance that Hitchcock's presumed errors offer to the Master's harmonies is their strange aptness to his work as *dis*harmonies.

That imperfectly hidden boom mike in *The Wrong Man*, for instance, will later be doubled in the "open" mike that grotesquely disfigures our view of Manny's face at Police Headquarters; the rhyme links the carceral apparatus to Hitchcock's filmmaking, thus suggesting that his liberal-minded movie is borrowing its technology from the police. Similarly, in *North by Northwest*, the little boy who inadvertently plugs his ears to muffle a gunshot that hasn't yet occurred harks back to a scene in the Oak Bar where a businessman Roger is about to meet mimes being hard of hearing before there is scarcely a syllable to hear. While the man's gesture proclaims an impairment that will soon affect Roger himself, when he fatally summons a hotel page whom he has failed to hear calling for "George Kaplan," the boy's has no narrative rationale whatsoever. Yet the visual field invites us to pair them for their suggestively synonymous enactments—the first figurative, the second literal—of "jumping the gun." They become symptoms, as such, of that classic overanticipation experienced by characters and viewers alike in the course of Hitchcockian suspense. Under the guise of continuity errors, then, both boy and boom mike exemplify what, following Stephen Booth, I'd call an "available but unmade pun." Visual equivalents of the dormant verbal play that Booth finds in words such as "hierarchy" (higher) and exegesis (Jesus), and the garden-variety adolescent hears in "titillate" and "hoary," they precipitate nonsensical associations that, however offensive to logic or taste, charge our rational perception with subversive, chaotic energy.[8] Hitchcock's cinema is full of such eye-puns, "unmade" in the sense that it falls to the viewer to do the making. Even if they are only the result of chance, no director is more alive to the uncanny dimension of chance than Hitchcock. As a character in a film by Claude Chabrol, the "French Hitchcock," aptly puts it, "Chance exists—and it is fantastic!" This book contends that, with their ostensible wrongness doubled by a potential rightness, so-called continuity errors in Hitchcock are a main source of his work's enigmatic richness.

This is not only because a given continuity error happens to chime with a given detail in the story; en bloc, the errors uncannily combine with the whole ethos of mistake, confusion, and nonsense that permeates Hitchcockian cinema, from its elaborate intrigues that never make sense on close inspection, to its perfectionistic protagonists foiled by slipups as little as a latchkey, to its general theology of original sin that puts everyone, and even everything, in the wrong. Hitchcock may not set out to commit a particular continuity error, but in his accident-driven Weltanschauung, any such error must be considered as waiting to happen, and when it does, feel not just stupidly out of place, but also eerily at home. These motley accidents, though narratively dysfunctional, have the odd capacity to bond, like open valences in chemistry, with stylistic motifs that lend them some of their own artistic necessity. Yet these bonds are wild, unstable; they neither facilitate stylistic homogeneity nor bring hermeneutic repose to the Too-Close Viewer who attempts to read them. In inviting us to *account* for the continuity errors, Hitchcock's style would not be pointing to a secret coherence that, once unveiled, makes the oeuvre whole, but rather to a teasing insistence on disjuncture that asks to be factored in even when it doesn't add up. Two films in particular, *Rope* (1948) and *The Wrong Man*, actively organize the interface between a story of mistake and the mistakes of storytelling as a knotty interpretative space. I call this organization Hitchcock's understyle.

Archive: The Wrong Hitchcocks?

I am a devout believer where Hitchcock is concerned: he is One, I confess, and the glory of his creation shines forth in *Jamaica Inn* (1939) no less than *Vertigo*. Accordingly, I am at liberty to worship him in any of his fifty-two manifestations; there simply are no wrong choices. And yet, while forms of hidden picturing are lying all over the place in Hitchcock, the impetus for wanting to *write* on them came almost entirely from the three films I treat in this book: *Strangers on a Train* (1951), *Rope*, and *The Wrong Man*. Why these films and not others? To anyone not myself, who was galvanized by it, my archive must appear, if not exactly marginal, a bit "off," drawing on Hitchcock's greatest period (the long '50s) but stopping just before *Vertigo* and the other universally acknowledged masterpieces in its wake.[9] Was there something about these three films, unlike the canonical "must-sees," that favored a less preempted perception, enabling the drift of too-close viewing away from what can't *not* be seen to what merely may be? Did this now-minor triad spare me from disburdening myself of the massive critical and cultural investment in the now-major works, which one can no more see with fresh eyes than the Mona Lisa? Or was it Hitchcock's unusually programmatic formalism in these three films (e.g., the "fascinating" crisscross pattern in *Strangers*, the continuous mobile camera in *Rope*, the neorealist relaxation of suspense in *The Wrong Man*) that promoted my narrative detachment? All I know is that if there were other or better choices, they were never mine to make. These films seemed to choose me; by whatever fatal attraction, they alone laid the traps I fell into with the sufficiently catalyzing thud. From which I conclude that my archive *is* a bit off—as necessarily decided by the chance circumstances of a particular person as is too-close viewing itself.

Book of Essays

This work is conceived as a "book of essays"; in the mythology of scholarly criticism, the phrase oxymoronically conjoins two warring formal realities. In the right corner stands the brawny objective Book, while in the left waits the slight subjective Essay. The Book dictates a rigorous "architectural" subordination of its parts to the unfolding of a governing argument. It achieves its objective effect by two linked renunciations: (1) authorial subjectivity is as self-starved as a boxer getting into fighting form; (2) shed in the same regimen, the aesthetic cannot do duty as an active or self-reflective element of the Book's own style and form—a pretty mug is just asking for it! The Book may encourage inventiveness qua thought-experiment, but not as an experiment in form. By contrast, the brevity of the Essay would never be confused with an efficient "chapter," any more than its freestanding attitude would make us think it was just that radically pared-down Book we call an "article." That is because the Essay gives broad play to the very impulses that the Book, or chapter or article, suppresses. The Essay welcomes the critic's moods, tones, and emotions, and its hospitality melts the matter at hand into something as fluidly "impressionistic" as, in the name of intellectual rigor, this critic is regularly censured for being. The converse is true, too. The Essay is so deeply permeated by the works of art of which it speaks that, as Adorno has put it, it simply cannot treat aesthetic matters unaesthetically. If the Book may be said to require a thinker who is never allowed to become a full-fledged writer, the Essay would insist on having a writer prevented by that very fact from being taken seriously as a thinker. In the US academy of my formation, the worst thing you could say about a book was that it was merely a collection of essays, a juvenile impostor donning a sage's beard; while the highest compliment you could pay to an essay was that it was really a small book, by which you meant that, deep down, it had abjured any undesirably indulgent form.

You will already have predicted my "defiant" sympathies: against the Goliath-Book, I take the side of the David-Essay. The three essays here are neither compacted little books nor well-fitting chapters in the arc of a bigger book's articulation. Each has been written as an independent contribution to the criticism on a given Hitchcock film. Intrinsically, despite a shared topic and practice, each imagines itself in the form of an *only child*, as the author's first, last, and sole word on hidden Hitchcock and too-close viewing. Cross-conversation between these bell jars is a perfunctory politeness at best. Even the author's style doesn't carry over as well as it should because, in the true Essay manner, it has made itself so porous to the subject matter that the particularity of a given film saturates the grain of the writing about it.

And yet two pressures bind the essays despite the logic of their fenced-off form. The one is that of collocation. Read alone, the essays wear the aspect of self-sufficient texts, but read alongside one another, they repeat themselves—not of course in their specific content, which is determined by the film under discussion, but as structurally similar trials in a quest to find hidden Hitchcock. In this respect, the quest, instead of proceeding cumulatively, seems to begin from scratch with every new film; as in a recurring dream, the same thing keeps happening, or failing to happen, to a Too-Close Viewer who never learns, or just keeps learning the same thing. Thus doubled and redoubled, the autonomous essay generates a form that exceeds it: a permutative *series*, in which this viewer appears to be performing a ritual, repeating a compulsion, and mimicking Hitchcock's auteurism (many works, one Work) all at once. Three being the minimally sufficient number for serial form, I stop there.

The other pressure—that of sequence—derives from the

same number. Triadic structure, no matter how equivalent its units, rarely fails to impose a plot; even the eternally co-present persons of the Holy Trinity bear a narrative relationship to one another: the Son is begotten by the Father and the Holy Spirit proceeds from the Father and the Son. And so here, each essay may be seen to highlight a distinct phase and mood in the game that the Too-Close Viewer has been summoned to play. The first essay, occasioned by *Strangers on a Train*, would present the Too-Close Viewer's inaugural "fall" into the game and, accompanied by astonishment and wonder, his preliminary exploration of its brave new world. By the time of his encounter with *Rope* in the second essay, he has become a seasoned player, puffed up with confidence in his ability to coax things out of hiding; no longer fazed by anything in this game, he imagines he will go on playing it forever. In the third essay, where he confronts *The Wrong Man*, a film that seems to him virtually *all* hidden pictures, and that, instead of reading *in toto*, he is able to read only in small decanted fragments, the euphoria has turned to discouragement, and the animation to depression; even in these small doses, we find him overwhelmed by the infinite fullness of the visual field, and by the radical discontinuity and inconsistency he meets with everywhere in it. Having seen enough to know he will never see enough, or will always be seeing too much, and abruptly seized by a longing to close his overburdened eyes at last, he seems on the verge of going, in Norman Bates's words, "a little bit mad." *Initiation, Proficiency, Defeat*: such would be the motto of this book-after-all, as it relates the vicissitudes of too-close viewing.

Hidden Pictures
(*Strangers on a Train*)

> Perhaps you read too much.
>
> Guy to Bruno in *Strangers on a Train*

Hidden Pictures

First, from *Strangers on a Train* (1951), something obvious, literally obstructing the way. The eponymous train is coming into Metcalf; Guy Haines is about to get off, and though it's early in the film, he's bearing considerable narrative momentum with his valise and tennis rackets. At Metcalf, he's supposed to meet his hateful wife, Miriam, about a divorce that would allow him to marry the more personable Ann Morton, but he has also just met Bruno Antony, a stranger on the train, who has broached a less civilized plan: Bruno will murder Miriam if, in an undetectable (because unmotivated) swap of killings, Guy will murder Bruno's tyrannical father. We are already savoring the delicious conviction that the psychopathic alternative will be the one to grip the rails. But now, all of a sudden, a man comes onto the station platform proposing to board the train at the same narrow door where Guy stands ready to leave it; the man's corpulence, not to mention a large contrabass that he is brandishing like a second paunch, magnifies the impediment. Yet between Guy

1.1 Hitchcock's dare: the manifest appearance.

and *this* stranger, not the slightest contact. Nimbly slithering around the fat man as if tracing the invisible but firm line of a cordon sanitaire, Guy makes sure to avoid any brush of the sort that has just made him so unexpectedly intimate with Bruno. Indeed, as he waves his valise in the air to avoid grazing the fat man's fat instrument, his rather theatrical courtesy seems less a sign of good manners than the subtle expression of an aversion. After he has detrained, moreover, the camera is neither so polite nor so subtle. Instead of following Guy on the narrative business, it lingers on the fat man as he hoists his bass, and then himself, up the stairs onto the train, its low angle emphasizing the mighty labor of his haunch as he ascends (figure 1.1).

Humiliated by both Guy's polite disregard and the camera's merciless observation, this surreal fatso is of course Alfred Hitchcock, the director of *Strangers on a Train*. I have been describing what is known as his *appearance* in the film. Every Hitchcock thriller stages such a moment, when, as Richard Allen puts it, "the flesh-and-blood director himself" enters the image, cutting a passing figure onscreen; but the *Strangers* appearance is exemplary in being perfectly unmissable.[1] No sooner does Hitchcock come forward onto the platform than every theatrical audience all over the world emits the pleased purrs, the complacent chuckles of its recognition; the communal gloating is as definitive of the cameo as is Hitchcock's own flesh and blood.[2] Even so, it remains a somewhat puzzling response. To judge by our swollen heads, one would suppose that Hitchcock had been trying to *escape* our attention rather than call it to a convention of his own devising. One would further suppose that other people in the audience, less clever than ourselves, fail to notice his appearance, even though (barring infants and aliens) such ignorant spectators are hard to come by. This appearance is no *secret*, no obscure reference for an elite; mass-culture spectators, we read only what has been made legible for that purpose. And yet we all feel as pleased as a child who has just discovered a hidden picture, and as knowing as the cinephile who, watching *Last Year at Marienbad* (1961), smiles to himself when he detects Hitchcock hovering in midair among the hotel guests (figure 1.2).

For though everyone in the theater may be familiar with Hitchcock's identity, this familiarity is not shared by anyone onscreen. It is in relation to these ignorant "persons of the fiction" that our feelings of superiority have been instigated and feel justified. As *whom*, after all, does Hitchcock appear in his films? Certainly, he never appears as anyone other than Hitchcock; he is never a character who bears another name, or even anonymously exercises the slightest narrative

1.2 Hitchcock at Marienbad.

function. As Anthony Shaffer put it, "He would be himself, but he wouldn't be anybody else."[3] Accordingly, we do not say, "There is a bassist played by Alfred Hitchcock," but "There is Alfred Hitchcock carrying a bass." Yet though the fiction never identifies its author as someone else, neither does it acknowledge him as *Hitchcock*. Guy Haines, for instance, is utterly—and to us, amazingly—oblivious to the fact he has just crossed paths with a film director as famous for his image as for the films regularly signed by that image. This is the self-contradiction intrinsic to the appearance: the fat man is nobody but Hitchcock, and yet Hitchcock is nobody but a fat man.

His fictional nonrecognition is absolute, universal. It is not just that he is unsightly among the beautiful people, or anonymous and shabby among the rich and famous. With no part to play, no narrative pertinence, he lacks social being altogether; and absent such relational traction, his embodiment has no more existential grounding than a ghost. (That is what Alain Resnais lets us understand in *Marienbad*'s faux-appearance, where the obese Hitchcock is shown defying gravity.) Paradoxically, Hitchcock's appearance in his films dramatizes his *invisibility* to their world; he arrives onscreen only to confirm this social death, and having done that, like a person who "knows when he is not wanted," he disappears to trouble us no more. That is why our own recognition of Hitchcock inevitably means patronizing him. Like gods, we seem to be giving him the only life he will ever know; like parents, we bestow on him the primal recognition that he seems able to get in no other way, and from no other source. "Yes," our complacent notice says to the fat man, "Your appearance to the contrary, you are truly Hitchcock the filmmaker. We love you for being him, and perhaps even more, for your self-abasing dependency on us to *see* that you are him."

Let me now bring forward another specimen of obviousness that comes even earlier in *Strangers*: the chance encounter between Guy and Bruno that gets the story going. If Hitchcock's appearance offered the obviousness of an obstruction, of something in the way of the story, this accident-waiting-to-happen—justly regarded as one of Hitchcock's most absorbing visual narrations—offers the obviousness of the way itself, of the narrative path that our attention is being directed to follow. The film famously begins by cross-cutting between two men's shoes, a pied pair walking leftward, and a plain pair walking to the right. The alternation accelerates, with suitable musical punctuation, and we expect it to culminate in a toe-on collision. Instead, it resolves in a shot that shows the men's shoes striding in the same direction, through the ticket gate and onto the train platform. But we are not disappointed, only further teased. The title has foretold an encounter between strangers "on a train," and it is this train that both pairs of shoes are now going to board, and whose departure is implied in the next shot, a low forward tracking shot along the rails. Unsurprisingly, the alternation resumes inside the train, and this time it reaches its promised end. The pied shoes again move left, until their owner, still invisible, sits down and crosses his legs. The plain shoes move right until their owner, also still unseen, follows suit; but in the process, his shoe kicks the other's across the aisle.

This is the moment we've been waiting for, and now the camera, as if it too had been kicked, shoots up from its low position on the floor and finally shows us something besides footwear: a brightly lit train car whose occupants, having sprouted heads and torsos, are busy talking, drinking, and playing cards. It is as if those touching shoes were the contact for an electric current that had turned everything on, including the narrative engine. For we immediately recognize the two men in the foreground as the film's stars and protagonists; and they waste no time striking up a conversation—"Aren't you Guy Haines? I'm Bruno, Bruno Antony"—chockful of exposition and suggested developments. Out of the womb of suspense, narrative is at last unmistakably delivered, healthy and full of beans; and after our drawn-out wait, we are the more pleasurably intrigued; the film is laying track.

We are unlikely, therefore, to pay attention to a small detail that emerges at the very moment when the suddenly upraised camera gives Guy and Bruno their first full registration. This is the book that Guy is holding, his train reading; on its back cover is the face of—Alfred Hitchcock, who is thus visible, if not actually seen, eight minutes before what we commonly take as his appearance (figure 1.3). There is no doubt about it; we get several more views of this book—the front cover as well as the back, and the spine too—and though no one has ever noticed it,[4] I did not find it impossible to identify. It is

1.3 Hitchcock's dare: the latent appearance.

Alfred HITCHCOCK'S *Fireside Book of* SUSPENSE, a collection
of mystery stories, published by Simon & Schuster in 1947,
that Hitchcock edited, annotated, and prefaced with an essay
called "The Quality of Suspense" (figures 1.4 and 1.5).

Let me note in passing that on discovering this book, I was
seized with a desire to possess it. It was as if the discovery
would not be verified, nor my satisfaction in it complete,
unless the thing in the film were also a thing close to hand
in my own home. Once I had got the book, though, the care
with which I scrutinized the jacket (which I was surprised
to observe was *red*, not gray as the black-and-white film
stock had rendered it) was more than matched by the care
with which I handled the book itself, so much more that it
almost seemed I was afraid to touch it. I soon felt a need to
insulate it; I put the book in a clear plastic zippered case, the
case in an archival box, and the box in the empty drawer of

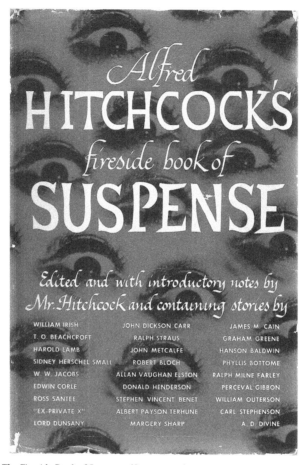

1.4 *The Fireside Book of Suspense* (front cover).

a locked cabinet where, I told myself, this precious deposit
would never get bruised against other books, or faded from
the sun, or stolen by—but here I grew bewildered, for who
would ever steal such a thing, a treasure whose value I was
the only one to recognize? Though I had purchased the *Fireside Book* to hold and examine whenever I pleased, somehow
what finally pleased me most was putting it away, out of sight
and out of reach.

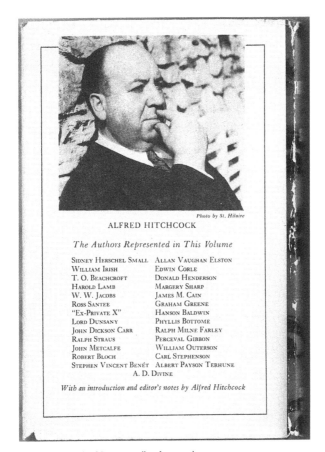

1.5 *The Fireside Book of Suspense* (back cover).

But I am jumping the rails. I return to the fact that Hitchcock makes, not one, but two appearances at the beginning
of *Strangers*—or rather, to the fact that this fact is precisely
what *doesn't* appear. Everyone thinks of the obvious or manifest appearance as the only one, and pays no attention to
the hidden or latent appearance at all. In one respect, of
course, both the manifest and the latent appearance do the
same thing: they sign the film as the work of "Hitchcock."
But they sign it with opposite implications. The manifest

appearance—of "the flesh-and-blood director himself"—
presumes that Guy doesn't know who Hitchcock is or what
he looks like, while the latent appearance—in the author
photo—implies that Guy is so fully appreciative of the Hitchcock brand—the name, the face, the suspense for which
these are synonyms—that, to while away the tedium of train
travel, he has chosen a book marketed on just that basis. And
instead of complimenting our ability to recognize Hitchcock
where no one else can, the hidden picture, when we do see it,
is bound to irk us. For whether we owe this finding to our own
(repeated, retarded, rewound) viewings, or to someone else's
information—perhaps, for most of you, my own—it is always a discovery of what we have missed, what we have been
set up to miss. We'd thought we were patronizing Hitchcock,
when all along it was he who was patronizing us; in smugly
discerning him, we were only being his dupes. He is not the
person we imagined—or rather, that person is not the author
we overlooked. Naïvely, we were content to find Hitchcock
in the flesh when we should have been looking for his image
on *film*, in that "still" which is the author photograph. And
now that we can no longer take the same pride in recognizing *Hitchcock*, we are no longer able to take the same pleasure in his film for recognizing *us* in our competence to read
it right.[5]

"You'll ruin everything with your neat little touches," says
Philip to Brandon in *Rope*, and the hidden picture here, neat
as a pin, and almost as hard to find, seems to be just such a
damaging touch: it mucks up the logic of the manifest appearance, and spoils the seigneurial pleasure, shared and
sure, we take in it. This is a signature that, like Sam Marlowe's

on his paintings in *The Trouble with Harry* (1955), is "not supposed to be readable" even if we end up being able to read it; and to confront its intended opacity, secrecy, or nonsense must radically disturb the straightforwardness of the film's art, along with the comfortable viewing practices we bring to it. Something thickens with this touch, and it's not the plot, which now begins racing forward like a train; it's the style, which, if we are to attend to it at all, must put the plot on pause, literally and otherwise.

But who would welcome such a violent application of the brakes? For if Hitchcock possesses the only great cinematic style with popular appeal, it enjoys this appeal on the basis of its beautiful clarity: the easy, immediate, and unbroken intelligibility of its purposes and means. As he tells us often enough, his trademark suspense depends on *sharing* information with the viewer. His camera is as directive as a teacher's pointer; it would designate *everything* noteworthy to the story, and *only* that. There never seems to be any money in letting our attention wander elsewhere on the blackboard. (During the most suspenseful sequence in *Strangers*, the camera is placed inside a gutter, where Guy's lighter has fallen onto a ledge; if you are sufficiently *dégagé* to look at anything here but Bruno's groping hand and the lighter it would grasp, you may be pardoned for thinking that nothing goes down a city sewer but a few dead leaves.) For all its brilliant withholding techniques, the style seems to harbor no deep secrets. As Andrew Sarris once put the point, "Hitchcock can be devious, but he is never dishonest"; we always feel we know what he is doing and why.[6] Such is the compact that the cameo has proved a winsome device for making explicit; it is the quasi-heraldic emblem of a style that would be—like itself—obvious, consistent, unmistakable. It anchors a game we derive considerable pleasure both from playing and from knowing how to play.

That is why the hidden picture, tampering with the readability of this emblem, making it a question or problem, has such power to unsettle; with this neat little touch, Hitchcock's whole style seems momentarily to cloud over, to surrender its classic functionality to an enigmatic density. In the manifest appearance, the story obligingly halts for recognition of Hitchcock as its author, then resumes its now-certified course. But in the hidden appearance, the narrative juggernaut leaves us no leisure for such recognition; its commanding progress almost ensures that Hitchcock's claim to authorship—in itself perfectly obvious—will be lost on us. And this effective incompatibility between narrative cognition and authorial recognition suggests that the "authorship" we *are* being asked to recognize is not the same thing as—and may even be at cross purposes with—the authorship of a narrative. Look closely at the author photo, and you will see Hitchcock holding his lips between his thumb and forefinger; the secret image embeds an emblem of secrecy itself.

To shift our self-congratulation, then, from the manifest to the latent appearance, as though, having now identified it, we could once again feel sophisticated and clever, would be to miss the implication of its latency, which is that the film might be hiding other objects, other "Hitchcocks," that are likewise visible *but not apparent.* Two other neat little touches may be observed in this connection. The first is that Guy's book is not the only book to be found on the train; Bruno rests his shoes on another, a paperback presumably his own, as he reclines on the compartment banquette (figure 1.6). All

1.6 Paperback under Bruno's feet.

we see of its cover are three differently sized lines of type, and all that can be distinctly read is the word SUSPENSE in the second and largest of these. But we've been given enough to know that the book is a kind of companion volume to the *Fireside Book*, a twinning that turns its author into Hitchcock by another name.

Or at least it would if he weren't in fact Hitchcock under his own name. On the hunch that this too was one of Hitchcock's anthologies, I found a paperback that bore a perfect typographic correspondence to the one lying under Bruno's heel (figure 1.7): "*Suspense Stories*, collected by Alfred Hitchcock," a Dell Mapbook (#367) published in 1950, the year before *Strangers*. (This too I bought, and all the rest.) The volume offers not only another Hitchcock signature, but also another iteration of the theme of the double that incessantly patterns the film's story and images. With the whole film in

1.7 *Suspense Stories.*

mind, one might see Guy and Bruno as having *chosen* the
Book of Hitchcock in an almost existentialist sense, though
the good Guy, in his bad faith, never gets around to reading
it, while the bad Bruno, said to "read too much" in the film
(and, more explicitly, in Patricia Highsmith's source novel,
to "read too many detective stories"), is good enough to do
Guy's dirty work. The point would be obvious if viewers were

1.8 The hidden picture interposed between Bruno and Guy.

allowed to get a good look at either book, and it is obvious anyway in the perfectly lucid formulations we find elsewhere in the film (as when Guy says, "I could strangle her," and the film cuts to a shot of Bruno's large hands). There is something, then, curiously beside the point here; if we see the hidden book, we must also perceive a sort of hiding for hiding's sake. For we can't think we've found a hidden meaning, or at least not a *meaningfully* hidden meaning, since we see more or less the same meaning elsewhere in plain view; we have merely found a hidden picture, whose concealment has no rationale. And compared to the *Fireside Book*, which reappers unobstructed at the end of the scene (figure 1.8), the partly seen Dell Mapbook has been so much further concealed that a successful attempt to identify it can no longer even *seem* particularly sharp-eyed; it must seem at once hugely pedantic and a tiny bit mad, the recondite fruit of a close reader whose attention has been diverted from the main line. For the film takes no responsibility for the game it has seduced us into playing; as a rule, Hitchcock's version of hidden pictures does not provide us with a list.

And things do not go more smoothly when it does. For the second neat little touch is that Hitchcock has made another "flesh-and-blood" appearance in *Strangers* in addition to the one on the platform. In *Hitchcock at Work*, Bill Krohn reports the following:

> After returning from location shooting in the East, the director told a Warners publicist that he had made a brief appearance as a librarian in the scene where Bruno accosts Guy and Ann in the Mellon Gallery. "It's such a small bit," he added, "I'm just likely to do another one before the film is finished" Rightly described as "small," Hitchcock's first appearance [first in order of filming, not in the film] survives as an out-of-focus rear projection behind Bruno at the Mellon lasting about a second, in which the director is nonetheless recognizable if you know to look for him.[7]

Recognizable if you know to look for him. You may find the phrase, as I did, a portal down the rabbit hole. For I still couldn't recognize Hitchcock even when, thanks to Krohn's source—Hitchcock himself—I did "know to look for him." As I watched and rewatched the scene, its periphery seemed to be swarming with stout middle-aged men, any one of whom might have been Hitchcock. I put them all under close inspection, like the police in *North by Northwest* hauling aside every porter in Union Station in hopes of finding Cary Grant, but equally in vain. Then, through a sudden accidental shift in perspective, no doubt caused by the sheer strain of the Morel-

lian attention I was according their blurred features and in-
distinct waistlines, I happened to observe the odd movement
with which one of these men walked on and off the scene. It
was different from the blandly purposive pacing of the others. Emerging from behind a pillar, the man seemed to be
walking sideways, even backward; and no sooner did he appear than, changing course and gait, he returned whence he
came. One glimpsed him from the back only, and his sudden
retreat came just in time to keep it that way, perhaps in order
to do so. Or had he sneaked a look at us before abruptly turning around? In either case, it was as though he were playing,
or showing himself playing, at hide and seek. What further
proof did I require? Here was Hitchcock beyond a doubt! And
under the impact of this revelation, Krohn's exasperating
locution—"recognizable if you know to look"—now spoke
only the plain truth, for once you find a hidden picture, it
seems always to have been there staring you in the face.

And yet, as I thought more about it, I came to realize that
the figure was not in fact *behind* Bruno; it was in front of
Bruno, right in his range of vision. Had Krohn—had I—got
it right? Doubt seized me again; I watched the scene another
time. And now I was struck by a man in black, seen over *Guy's*
shoulder, but also emerging from behind a pillar, who walks
quickly offscreen. At the moment he does so, Guy looks ner-
vously to the side, a synchrony suggesting that Guy may have
seen him out of the corner of his eye, or (Hitchcock characters often seem to possess such organs) with eyes in the back
of his head. The man is filmed in profile, and his dark cloth-
ing combines with the lighting to make him a virtual shadow
picture, an effect that evokes the self-silhouetting Hitchcock
delighted in and would soon trademark on *Alfred Hitchcock
Presents*. Which, then, was the genuine Hitchcock—the one

in silhouette or the one playing peekaboo? Or was there a third possibility I had not yet made out . . . ?

I recalled—I relived—the demoralized state I had often known while playing hidden pictures as a child. The game distressed me by what I experienced as a never-ending *embarras du choix*. First, every bulbous oblong discernible in the foliage, clouds, or mountain ridges would look to me like the hidden spoon; though the list unambiguously stated that there was only one, I seemed to see a hundred. Then, having at last decided on a winner and colored it in with my red crayon, I discovered that the other spoon-nominees did not recede into the background from which I had conditionally isolated them, but continued demanding my attention just as aggressively as they had done before. They *still* looked suspiciously like spoons, or—since that was now supposed to be impossible—like something else in hiding that I hadn't yet identified. And so with the other hidden objects on the list: my eventual identifications, instead of relieving my initial confusion, only made it less real, more hallucinatory. Hence, finally, when I was done finding everything, the original tableau—the "big picture" with its strong motivic unity—wasn't simply pockmarked with irrelevant spoons, paperclips, and catcher's mitts; it had dissolved into an infinite tracery of possible hiding places for objects I had not discovered and could not be sure even existed. The game never felt over, especially—and most creepily—when it was supposed to be.

But again I digress, unless all this may offer a way of thinking about the unnerving force that the Hitchcock appearance acquires as it moves among "obvious," "secret," and "undecidable" modes. It is, after all, a common experience in watching Hitchcock to suspect his presence in *every* man—

and even in some women—over a certain age and weight.[8] Not only are there many such suspects in the films, but they tend to exhibit characteristic formal features of the classic Hitchcock appearance: they obtrude into the frame from the side, often passing in front of the protagonist, or look straight at the camera, defying narrative purpose. *Strangers*, in spite or because of the obviousness of the platform appearance, seems especially rich in what might be called Hitchcock appearances without Hitchcock,[9] and the structural similarities between the phony Hitchcocks and the real one ensure that, no matter how many times we see the film, it will always be affirming that Hitchcock is one man and many men; that he appears but once and is on the verge of appearing all the time; that we will certainly find him and may just miss him.

Another way to "find Hitchcock" in his films, of course, is to identify one or more of his characters as an author surrogate—a stratagem that has enjoyed a tenacious hold on Hitchcock criticism from Robin Wood and William Rothman forward. Up to a point, finding the surrogate carries on the game enjoined by the cameo convention, but it is also an attempt to put an end to what is frustrating about the game, by refusing its mere formalism and harnessing its identificatory imperative to useful thematic service. For if we identify Hitchcock as the supernumerary walking backward in the Mellon Gallery, nothing in particular need follow from the fact; indeed, it would be hard to make *anything* follow from this discovery that was commensurate with its inconsequence. But if we find Hitchcock embodied in, say, Bruno (the evil mastermind), or Guy (the cynical arriviste), or even Barbara Morton (Ann's sister, the connoisseur of murder mysteries played by Hitchcock's own daughter Patricia), then the floodgates of meaning are opened to irrigate everyone's glibbest discourse; in being identified *with* a character, even partially, Hitchcock becomes comprehensible *as* a character, with motives and a mission, sympathies and a heart of darkness. Under the aegis of the cameo, we seek Hitchcock as part of a formal observance whose emptiness, sooner or later, afflicts us with hermeneutic *tristesse*; in the name of the surrogate, by contrast, we not only find Hitchcock, but also, having done so, *we find out what he means.* Replete with sense, with import, the surrogate compensates for the cameo, which is empty of any meaning extrinsic to the sheer game of looking for it.[10]

Why, then, you may ask, would anyone engage in the abstruse and absurd game of hidden pictures, whose recessiveness ensures its invisibility to most viewers and threatens to brand the others with its own marginality? But it is not my claim that Hitchcock's hidden pictures are *worthy* of our attention; they must seem all the more perverse and trivial for covering in such elaborate secrecy what can be—and elsewhere is—presented openly. They degrade our attention even in the quasi-chemical sense of breaking it down. Identifying them encourages a pointillist indifference to the "overall picture" in which they are hidden, a jokey dismissal of the film's more obvious, important, and attention-sustaining themes. And as I have already indicated, "pleasure" is not a very apt name for the affect these hidden pictures induce in one who is seriously—that is to say, naïvely—open to looking for them. But if there is no reason why anyone *should* engage in this game, there is a reason why some people *do*, and why everyone *could*, and that is its undeniable persistence throughout Hitchcock's work. Sooner or later, in one form or another, it is impossible not to stumble on evidence of this secret style that, once we suspect its existence, threatens to spoil the style famous for having no secrets.

Charades

It is tempting to regard the author-metaphor that the *Fireside Book* smuggles into *Strangers* as a genial prophecy of the French auteurism that would make Hitchcock its hero only a few years later. But in the work of the critics writing for *Cahiers du cinéma* during the late 1950s, the metaphor functioned very differently. On the one hand, the term "auteur" served to ennoble directors with a preeminently literary prestige, equating them not with composers or painters, but with the authors of poems, plays, novels: texts. On the other hand, nothing made a director less eligible to bear this literary title than symptoms of "literature" in his work. Truffaut excoriated "scenarists' films" where the *metteur en scène* was merely, as he witheringly put it, "the gentleman who adds the pictures" to literate adaptations.[11] And prompted by the same animus, Rohmer went so far as to condemn Rossellini himself "for having given too much to the literary objects he admires and for having sacrificed a bit of the tradition of Gance and Eisenstein to the false gods of Caldwell."[12] A true auteur's vision of the world could only be expressed through a mastery of tracking shots, depth of field, montage, and other strictly cinematic techniques. This auteur was *comparable* to an author, as fully in control of his material; but he was never *like* him in having a literary orientation or in understanding cinema on the model of the written word. Because English imported the trope, we can distinguish the (film) auteur from the (book) author, but for the *Cahiers* critics who originated it, "auteur" remained a perfect figure of speech; you could only be called one if you weren't one.

In *Strangers*, however, the author-metaphor is wholly literal and unabashedly literary. It is as the author of an actual book that the director advances his claim to be an equivalently authoritative artist in film.[13] In contrast to the *Cahiers* critics who made him the auteur par excellence—in contrast, too, to his own later pronouncements to them regarding "pure cinema"—Hitchcock here suggests that his cinematic art may be seen as *deriving from a book*. Indeed, his paper-thin head shot precedes his fuller and rounder incarnation on the platform almost as if he had stepped off his own back cover, and with him, no less fantastically, the Hitchcock suspense thriller that Guy was proposing to enjoy in fireside-like comfort and safety had also come off the page to envelop the hero in its trammels. One is weirdly reminded of that classic opening of adaptations where we see the words of the source-novel's first page fading into the film's first scene, as if come to life.

But what "words," you might object, when Hitchcock's book is mainly represented by a photo in which the author, clasping his lips, designates an inviolable muteness? Yet though one can hardly verbalize the virtually blank secret being kept here, one can hardly *but* verbalize the gestural code for keeping it: "mum's the word," "my lips are sealed," "silent as the grave," and so on. Theatrically emphatic, the mime announces a *charade*, a riddling gesture or tableau covertly determined by a verbal expression that it is asking us to supply. In its sheer ostentation, let it stand as an emblem—the only sort of emblem we are likely to get—of the game of charades that is played unannounced in Hitchcock, and whose very riddles are posed in secret, hidden under narrative camouflage until someone, accidentally falling into the game, simultaneously sees and solves one.

On the day—or rather night—of my own initiation, it was too late to watch *Strangers* "responsibly"; only half-awake, I began to half-dream over the film, following the train of whatever associations crisscrossed my mind. Far be it from me to demean this semi-unconscious mode of viewing; it is sometimes responsible for our closest—most intimate and most precise—readings of a work's details; but as, most of the time, it produces entirely unusable irrelevancies, I have never *chosen* to adopt it. Anyway, in this woolgathering state, I happened to be struck by Hitchcock's contrabass, and remembered how frequently his appearance in other films also makes him out to be musical.[14] This recurring motif seemed to enjoy a particular pertinence in *Strangers*, since when Guy bypasses Hitchcock, he is on the way to Miller's Music Store, where Miriam works. According to the writing on its front windows, the store sells "Records, Radios, and Musical Instruments," and amid the grand piano, clarinet, accordion, banjo, guitar, and drums visible on the premises, a bass would not be out of place. My irresistible thought: since Hitchcock gets on the train that Guy has just left, might not he also have left the music store where Guy is just about to go? They are, after all, pictured as *crossing paths*, and if we are allowed to think of Hitchcock as joining Bruno, who we already know is a fan, we may also imagine him as having just parted from Miriam, who we soon learn is fond of music. None of this, I knew, had any narrative reality; it was sheer connotative filigree.

I was further struck—indeed felt almost personally hailed—by the cast album of *Carousel* hanging conspicuously in Miller's window, which linked the music shop to my old passion for Broadway musicals and linked both to the film's own merry-go-round. And there, in fact, Miriam's Hitchcockian affinity with music was reaffirmed. "Hey, let's sing, come on!" she enjoined her two beaux as all three boarded this carousel and broke into "The Band Played On," as they might have performed a chorus of "June Is Bustin' Out All Over" or "A Real Nice Clambake." Even Bruno, already in pursuit, couldn't resist joining in from his horse behind them—nor could I, in a similarly low voice, watching it all from my couch. Bruno's stalking no doubt threw a shadow over Miriam's laughing rendition of "the poor girl would shake with alarm," but it did not affect my rising piano-bar spirits; I knew it was a false alarm: Miriam would not shake when she was strangled, but fall in a swoon, as if Bruno were romantically embracing her.

But then the singing was done, and Miriam was insisting on a boat ride through the Tunnel of Love; the carousel music had changed to "Baby Face." Whether I regretted that the impromptu sing-along had ended, or was still obeying Bosswoman Miriam's earlier directive, or had otherwise determined, on this strange train of associations, to be an actual passenger, I now began mouthing the words to the new song, which I knew quite well:

> Baby face
> I'm up in heaven when I'm in your fond embrace
> I didn't need a shove
> 'Cause I just fell in love
> With the cutest baby face!

But just as I sang to myself, "I didn't need a shove," the boatman onscreen took up a long pole and—*gave Bruno's boat a shove* (24:58–25:04). I did not believe my eyes. The man was no longer simply helping Bruno debark, as he had done in my numerous previous viewings of *Strangers*; now, he was also literalizing the words of the song, words that, never heard in the film, and supplied only by my memory, had nonetheless secretly shaped his gesture. With my recognition of this fact, the image itself altered, doubled into the old familiar host-image that had just vanished and the fantastic new charade-image that had now taken its place. For even though the new image was identical to the old, it did not *look* like it. I had just found another kind of hidden picture—or rather, as I had done no searching, it had found me. And this picture was far weirder than if the prophesy of "the poor girl would shake with alarm" had been realized in an image of Miriam trembling; for that image would have done no more than *illustrate* the words that had foreshadowed it.[15] Here, the boatman was literalizing words that were never meant to be taken literally. The song's "I didn't need a shove" does not envision rough physical pushing; it is, as more than one Hitchcock character likes to say, just an expression.[16]

I fell into my discovery by accident, but like all accidents, this one had no sooner befallen me than it acquired the fatedness of a thing waiting to happen. The coincidence of word and image—the whole concatenation of associations—seemed far too exact not to have been designed by Hitchcock, planted there like a land mine to lie inert and invisible until either it self-destructed with the last surviving copy of *Strangers on a Train*, or someone should trip over it and explode it into visibility—someone who bore the name Miller, knew the lyrics to "Baby Face," had fallen into a daze, or enjoyed some other nonce qualification. But designed, planted for what purpose? The charade's solution ("need a shove") adds absolutely nothing to our understanding of the story.

What interpreter would stoop to decide whether queer Bruno *does* need a shove into the heterosexual tunnel of love—or, in his compulsively "driven" state of mind, *doesn't*? But even if the point were less idle than it is, no possible thematic utility could mitigate the shock of the charade's sudden visibility as such.

For it is not just that the charade is blindingly apparent where its existence had been unsuspected. Its sudden prominence also triggers the narrative's simultaneous *waning*. The fictional world is flattened into a pretext for constructing a trivial if amusing picture puzzle; and though the picture puzzle is necessarily telling us *something*, it is emphatically *not* telling the story that has been engaging us. Though composed of moving images that are all justified by this story, the charade only becomes legible as a motionless tableau with its own independent raison d'être; in thus stemming the narrative flow, it suspends suspense itself.

What's more, a disturbance inheres in the sheer form of the charade as the visual literalization of a verbal figure. Unlike a simple illustration, in which word and image are understood to correspond, the riddling nature of a charade depends on their incommensurability; and once a charade has been solved, image and expression alike lose their spontaneously given obviousness. The image, at first banal, now looks eerily disassociated, a literalization that has failed to catch the *sense* of the expression it materializes, while, in the light of this materialization, the expression, which we knew perfectly well how to use, also feels dislocated from its meaning, like any figure we think about too literally. Although a charade can be neither constructed nor deciphered without a certain, often considerable wit, its end-effect is to make image and expression seem idiotic: two equally nonsensical moments in a comedy of misrepresentation. Again, for what purpose would Hitchcock introduce a charade here? Would its only point be, saboteurlike, to set off this tiny explosion of pointlessness in a film that is otherwise shoved along by its highly efficient plot mechanisms?

Or to set off, in our now altered state, a whole string of such absurd explosions, occurring not just in a backwater, around a minor plot notation, but at major narrative junctures, on the train itself? Call to mind again the juncture of all such junctures in the film, the seed encounter between Pied Shoes and Plain Shoes. After being teased and toyed with, we grasped that the contact between them would occur once, following Pied Shoes' example, Plain Shoes had crossed his legs. In that same moment—also the moment to which the secret appearance of Hitchcock as charade-player has been timed—we might now also grasp, gasping and gaping with the knowledge, that our suspense has just come to coincide with a literalization of one of suspense's hoariest figures: we actually *are* "waiting for the other shoe to drop"! Likewise, it now becomes almost impossible to bear the suspense of Bruno groping for the lighter, or of Guy grabbing the poles while grappled by Bruno on the merry-go-round, without having a mental picturization—I borrow the term from Norman Bates—of how "gripping" all this is meant to be. We further see, among other nonsense literalizations, that the shot along the rails offers us a tracking shot of tracks; that the shots of the tennis game punningly correspond to shots in the game; that the popcorn machine, the Ferris wheel, and the merry-go-round are all wonderland resizings of cameras, reels, and projectors.[17] These may not all be equally persuasive examples of Hitchcock's pictionary; just as the hidden pictures range from obvious to secret to speculative, so the charades are now incontrovertible, now merely likely, now, like the author photo that emblematizes them, abidingly enigmatic. *Strangers* is riddled with such riddles, what, in her own wonderland, Alice aptly calls "out-of-the-way things"; once you find the rabbit hole, it's unbelievable what's down there!

Touch Tag

But can any of it be brought back above ground? The question is all the more germane now that my objective account of the hidden pictures has mutated into a subjective experience of them, and my critical essay into a fantastic tale à la Poe. In order that this doubleness may at least be better understood, let me say a few last words about the practice that has determined it. This is the practice of what I'll call too-close reading.

As the name is meant to insinuate, too-close reading would be, transposed to the study of film, a late, deviant iteration of the "close reading" pursued in literary criticism after the Second World War. It deserves to be called "too close" on several accounts. It has abandoned the sense of overall proportion that gave the New Criticism its Attic shape, and dispensed with the evenhanded stance that was once its fair attitude. Too-close reading no longer aims at offering a "reading," the interpretation of "the work as a whole" that was close reading's rationale and telos. Instead, it is drawn to details that, while undeniably intricate, are not noticeably important— little particulars that, though demonstrably *meant*, never strike us as deeply *meaningful*. Nor is too-close reading concerned with pinning down the meaning or import that eludes us; "close, but no cigar" is its very watchword. Unlike classic close reading, it does not "illuminate" the text, but only brings out its shadowy and even shady quality.[18] If it is good for anything, then, too-close reading is good for measuring a film's drive to futility, a perverse force that is, in Hitchcock's case, considerable. The effort of what I've called his secret style is to create—discreetly, for true initiates—an alternative universe in which the celebrated storytelling, suspense, and entertainment of the manifest style all get derailed.

"For true initiates"? There remains, therefore, to observe one last aspect of too-close reading: namely, that, whether eagerly like Bruno, or merely tractably like Guy, it acquiesces in *an undue intimacy*. The practitioner of too-close reading is never as lonesome as he might appear, nor his findings as singular; he is always partnered with an author-text to which he can't help getting, in this relational sense as well, inordinately close. It is through consenting to this undue intimacy, with its blurred boundaries and invaded spaces, that too-close reading acquires its weird psychic density. This is also why, when the author-text is Hitchcock, it is well-suited to register another curious hidden truth about his cinema: it comes *too close*, closer than, as cinema, it should.

Hitchcock's manifest appearance in *Strangers on a Train*, for instance, does not simply realize our well-trained desire to see Hitchcock; it also, more monstrously, issues a fantasmatic invitation to touch him. The invitation is broached in the very taboo *against* touching him that determines Guy's politely channeled repulsion; and it is continued in the sheer aggression with which the camera proceeds to put Hitchcock's fat ass "in our face": a taunting dare to kiss it.[19] In the latent appearance, moreover, the prohibition on touching Hitchcock has been lifted ante factum: at the moment we first see Guy, he is laying an oblivious finger on the Untouchable's cheek (see figure 1.3). And he must have put it there *just before* he crossed his legs, so that his pedal contact with Bruno, which literally kicks off the entire story, is itself a jerk reflex, the extension and downward displacement of his digital fondling of Hitchcock. It is as if Guy had touched Hitchcock, and were now strangely bound to him, under pressure of the idiom "hand and foot." Conversely, Bruno's overfamiliarity would be merely carrying on from the intimacy already established in this double first touch—a touch that his own remarkably large hands and feet, as they pound and trample Guy on the carousel, may be considered a last means of returning. Recall the Too-Close Reader's desire to handle, if not the actual Hitchcock, the actual Hitchcock book; how quickly he found himself putting it away, sensing that his too-closeness to Hitchcock had found its obscene truth in Hitchcock's too-closeness to him. The dream of touching Hitchcock—of probing his secret parts—had become indistinguishable from the nightmare of being touched by him, of being likewise deeply probed. English used to have a word for this horror: *thrilling*; it meant penetrating, or piercing.

Even at the obvious narrative level, of course, the touch typically implies violence and violation; Guy kicks and slugs, Bruno throttles and stomps, and Barbara herself, vigorously brushing off the face powder she has spilled on Detective Hennessy's trousers, comes ominously near his crotch. Even lighter and presumably more loving forms of touch carry a hint of trauma. When Ann runs up to kiss him, Guy calls her a "brazen woman" and redoes the kiss with himself in control; and having just had his hands manicured by his mother, Bruno compulsively nuzzles *her* hands, as if to bargain for a truce. But all such represented touches are not too close for our comfort as spectators; as befits the aesthetic *enjoyment* of fear, we observe them from a safe place.[20]

It is in the too-close proximity to Hitchcock's secret style, however, that one appreciates its ambition to abolish that safe place, to turn "the touch" from something the film embodies to something the film performs on the bodies watching the film. I am indifferent to whether *Bruno* needs his prodding or not, but I am intensely "thrilled" by the prodding the charade gives *me*, whether I need, want, or like it. No doubt, to call this overintimizing effect a "touch" is to employ a figure of speech; but it is one that Hitchcock liked to use himself, and as with other figures of speech once they enter his cinema, it doesn't stay buried in the grave of dead metaphors. In *Strangers*, his "touch" comes alive not only in the finger-to-lip pose he strikes in the book-jacket photograph, but again in the contrabass he carries onto the train; both appearances literalize touch as the sign, the means, and the end of his art.

Charade-wise, though, these literalizations of touch are secreted. If the photograph can just be glimpsed, the bass, with its pluckable strings, cannot be seen at all; what is visible is only the canvas case that hides its haptic powers. Hitchcock's supremely visual cinema seems to be similarly shrouding, within its seemingly distanced visuality *as* cinema, a more basic aspiration to literal, actual touching. Notoriously, the director imagined a day when his audience would be implanted with electrodes and he could jolt them into fright or mirth, as he chose, merely by touching different buttons. This fantasy, as Lee Edelman has recognized, bespeaks less a "futuristic anticipation" on Hitchcock's part than an "actual understanding" of what his cinema already is; and the metaphor is not much different from that implied in *Strang-*

ers of playing the audience like a musical instrument.[21] But more remarkable than their common sadism (which, so grossly overplayed, is more ironic than cruel) is the fact that both metaphors entirely eliminate visual mediation. It is as though, however elaborate and indeed indispensable, such mediation were felt to be standing in the way of the more basic project of touching, which it could at best, therefore, express obliquely—in certain peripheral and barely perceptible details that only one holding the object too close had a chance of catching. At a cost, to be sure. For the touch that precipitates the story in *Strangers on a Train* is nothing next to the film's own more intimate touches, as they pierce through the too-thin skin of the too-close spectator. Thanks to their secret reach, Hitchcock's hidden pictures—by which I finally mean Hitchcock's hidden *motion* pictures—get under this skin, and deep in the heart, like nothing else in cinema. Does that mean I am in love with Hitchcock? I only know that I am hopelessly attached.

Understyle (*Rope*)

C'est pire qu'un crime; c'est une faute.

Talleyrand

Why the Perfect Crime Is Never Perfect

"Brandon, you don't think the party's a mistake, do you?" That is the question Philip puts to his lover at the beginning of Alfred Hitchcock's *Rope* (1948). Only minutes before, the two have strangled their old classmate, David Kentley, just for the sake of killing. Now, compounding the outrage, they are about to throw a party for the victim's parents, fiancée, and friends; the venue is the very apartment, their own, where the murder took place and the corpse lies stiffening, soon to begin rotting, at the bottom of a handsome antique cassone. Philip has every reason to be apprehensive. The party *is* a mistake; at the very least it increases the risk (otherwise nil) that their perfect crime will be exposed; in addition, Brandon has dared put on the guest list a certain Rupert Cadell, their former teacher and "the one man," Philip avers, "most likely to suspect."

But Brandon will have none of this worry. "No," he replies, stammering with exhilaration, "the party's the inspired finishing touch to our work. Uh, i-it's more—it's the signature of the artist. Uh, not having it would be like, uh, uh—." Lov-erlike, Philip completes his sentence: "like painting the pic-ture and not hanging it?" Brandon laughs off the pun, but it makes a point that would be grasped immediately by any aficionado of classic murder mysteries. There what is called a "perfect crime" is not merely an *undetected* crime but, more important, an *aestheticized* one. To kill for the sake of killing might make one a hero in Nietzsche-esque philosophies; but it is an insufficient condition for achieving that higher, more complex form of futility which is art for the sake of *art*. As the self-respecting author of an art murder, Brandon cannot simply get away with it; he must lay on the killing what he calls "touches": superfluous refinements of design whereby the criminal deed becomes an artistic work. While, to Philip, Rupert is "the one man most likely to suspect," to Brandon, he is "the one man who might appreciate this from our angle, the artistic one." And though the guests are "a pretty dull crew," the party will be "the most exciting of all time" with David's moldering corpse on hand to enrich, compostlike, the crew's labored banalities with unsuspected double meaning.[1]

It is in the art murder's twin status as "perfect crime" and "work of art" that its self-undoing lies. As an instance of perfection, the crime must be, in Brandon's expression, "an immaculate murder," without stain or other evidence to incriminate its author. To be an example of art, though, it must be marked with an intention, even a solicitation, to be recognized as one. In the art murder, then, perfection and art are radically at odds in their relation to the necessity of a signature. That is why most stories of the perfect crime, like *Rope* and Hitchcock's later *Dial M for Murder*, are really sto-ries of the perfect crime's failure; like so many fingerprints, those accumulated artistic touches eventually yield the forensic clues that give the game away. The recognition that the *artful* crime must do everything to secure, proves in the end but another name for the detection that the *perfect* crime has been designed to eschew.

"You'll ruin everything with your neat little touches," Philip remarks to Brandon.[2] "Neat," we'll see, isn't quite the word; but, artistically speaking, who would deny that Brandon's macabre touches have, in his own words, a "wonderful," even "brilliant" quality? When he offers David's father some first editions bundled with the same rope that choked David, the device is worthy of the Jacobeans. Still, as Philip also remarks, "it's a clumsy way of tying them." The objection, though obviously feigned to conceal his shock at the rope's new use, ends up having an uncanny validity. "You were right, Philip," says Rupert when he returns to the apartment with the rope in hand. "The books *were* tied clumsily." He implies that, in contrast to the efficient tautness of the rope-as-noose, the rope-as-harness came loose and caused the books to spill out; and we will see other books, as if re-enacting this undoing, scatter to the floor when he opens the cassone. Wonderful in embellishing but clumsy at concealment, neat in conception but ruinous when executed, Brandon's little touches may indeed be called "finishing": they crown the artwork while spoiling the crime.

The Case of the Canting Candle

Just as Philip is asking Brandon whether "the party is a mistake," Hitchcock's camera drifts over the dining table's nicely developing symmetry: two three-branched candelabra flank a floral centerpiece, with the silverware spaced evenly around. But the drift discloses a conspicuous imperfection:

2.1 The canting candle.

one candle, in contrast to its five companions, is drooping from its socket (figure 2.1). We notice this lopsided candle right before Philip pronounces the word "mistake," which almost seems to be captioning the image; and yet, plainly, this cannot be the mistake he has in mind. Is it even a mistake at all? It marks no character's failed intention, but only a haphazard contingency, like the bicycle that sometimes falls (but doesn't *always* fall) in *I Confess* (1953). And though we can't miss the candle, Hitchcock's camera is curiously roundabout in noting it. It does not zoom in on the candle or single it out with a quick shot, as it would typically do in his other work; instead it pans across the entire table and lets us catch the candle in passing. The movement seems a bit diffuse, not pointed enough to justify the apparent point. A further, more pronounced indecisiveness may be observed when the camera pulls back to reframe Brandon and Philip behind the

2.2 The canting candle "marginalized."

table. Even as it isolates the deviant candle at the edge of the frame, it joggles back and forth with a tremor that makes the emphasis oddly dubious (figure 2.2).

Still, in the exhilarating perfectionist air of the apartment, I find this sagging candle a serious enough source of irritation. I want the droop to be recognized and righted. Having seen what Philip and Brandon should see but don't, I wait for their knowledge to catch up with mine; and so I enter the classic state of Hitchcockian suspense. It is of course suspense of the mildest, most minor kind: only a well-laid table is at stake, and my wait is neither long nor anguished. Like a practiced hostess or decorator, Brandon no sooner sees the candle than he instinctively begins correcting its posture. At first, he simply tries to screw the candle back into position, in vain. Then, more ingeniously, he applies his lighter to the candle bottom and drips molten wax into the socket. Success!

60

2.3 Differently crooked.

Reset in this natural cement, the candle is secured. And secu-
rity comes with a bonus: the satisfyingly literary touch that
consists of righting the "wrong" candle by lighting it from
the wrong end. Two wrongs make a right after all.

Yet when this aesthetico-orthopedic operation is over, the
candle is still out of plumb; it has merely become differently
crooked, tilting to the right rather than the left (figure 2.3).
This new deviation is less marked, but I, whom this mute
piece of business has turned into a policeman of perpendic-
ularity, find it more grating than the old and am gripped by a
keener suspense. I again want it recognized and righted, but
my investment in the matter begins to feel compulsive. On
remarking the first deviation, I was positive I had made a per-
tinent observation and merely waited for Brandon to make
it, too; on remarking the second, which requires a finer perception, I am still certain of what I have *seen*, but I am unsure

2.4 Decay's monogram.

whether it is meant to be *observed*. For Brandon seems not to give it a glance, let alone a thought. No sooner has he completed his botched handiwork than he is overwhelmed by a fresh burst of artistic inspiration: he will serve the supper not on the table, but from the cassone. "It's brilliant," says the author of this gruesome new touch. "It's making our work of art a masterpiece."

And indeed, the touch dazzles by its near-oneiric economy. The improvised sideboard will condense three incipient processes of rot—the food spoiling on top, the guests digesting alongside, and the corpse putrefying within—in a gratifyingly misanthropic scene of man devouring man. In addition, this scene will enact a psychotically clever charade in which the question bound to be on everyone's lips—what happened to David Kentley?—will find its tacit answer in the materialization of his initials as a state of *decay* (figure 2.4).[3]

2.5 Candle still out of kilter.

Who would marvel that Brandon, overwhelmed by the sheer richness of his conceit, can no longer be bothered with an out-of-kilter candle? In yet another coincidence of art and mistake, of the touch and the flaw, his brainstorm has come upon him as a grandiose compensation for the minor imperfection that thus goes uncorrected (figure 2.5).

It now occurs to me that my own attention to the candle may have become nicer than the film is prepared to reward. I may be looking *too* closely at it, and, in consequence of this fixation, find myself exiled—alone, eccentric, "touched"—from the community of spectators to which I had confidently belonged only seconds before. In trying so hard to be the good spectator, have I really become a bad one? But no, not quite. After Brandon, himself transported, carries off the candelabrum to the cassone, he suddenly gives the candle

2.6 Righting the candle a second time.

a push to the left; my observation has been relevant after all (figure 2.6).

With this fresh proof that the candle is worth the game, I find less reason than ever to cease paying attention to it. I am compelled to notice, then, that Brandon's corrective push has no discernible effect; the candle retains the same off-angle bearing (figure 2.7). Faced with this ever more insistent deviancy, I feel ever more intensely annoyed. What will Brandon do now? To my dismay, he does nothing; he sensibly lets the matter go and carries on with the more pressing business of conveying the rest of the table setting to the cassone. Still more demoralizing, Hitchcock's camera, as if dismissing the matter on similar grounds (the story must not be kept waiting!), moves from a frontal framing of the candelabra to a lateral one, so that all six candles appear in single file and any

2.7 The candle righted again but still not right.

deviation from the perpendicular is minimized if not oblit-
erated (figures 2.8–2.10). So a Japanese fan might fold into a
slender bar of slats, or an image be anamorphically torqued
beyond recognition. Literally sidelined, the whole question
of the candle is now formally abandoned. What's wrong with
this picture will stay wrong, and it is not going to matter.

But in my present state, the persistence of an imperfection
that *was once, but will no longer be recognized* is almost intol-
erable. Not only has the lady vanished; a sane person will
never be supposed to have seen her in the first place. Merely
by following the film's lead, I have become more obsessive
and perfectionistic than Brandon, who boasts, "I would never
do anything unless I did it perfectly," or even Hitchcock, already in 1948 enjoying the reputation of a master who can
do no wrong. Still heeding the old injunction to attend to
the candle, I can't help defying the new injunction to forget

2.8–2.10 The candles collapsing into single file.

about it; slavish obedience has made a mutineer of me. Even in Hitchcock's new, neutralizing framing, the file of candles straggles a bit, and I readily spot the deviant candle by its greater height, greenish hue, and (to me) still glaring slant (figure 2.11). As for the other five candles in the lineup—the ones that had formed the standard against which I perceived the original deviation—these too begin to irk me with their irregular spacing and different heights; whether erect or tilting, pristine or encrusted with drippings, they *all* look awful. It is as though Hitchcock had craftily slipped me a perfectionist's monocle, which, having glued itself to my eyeball the moment I raised it, could never be removed. Through this accursed prosthesis, I am condemned to see nothing but niggling flaws. The film has barely begun and my best, my freshest attention has already been captured by sheer captiousness.

As if to insist on the necessity of putting the candle out of

2.11 Even in single file, the canting candle stands out.

mind, the camera now puts the candelabra out of sight. Indeed, it puts everything out of sight in a sudden eclipse of vision, a blackout on Brandon's back. This is one of *Rope*'s five
so-called hidden cuts. I will have more to say about these later
on, but just now I am too impatient to talk about the sight that
greets my bemonocled eye not a minute on the other side of
this first one. The murderous lovers are just where the blackout left them, resetting the buffet. Philip starts in on moving
a pile of books by the cassone to the dining table, where, as a
pretext for the new serving arrangement, they are to be laid
out for easy perusal by David's collector father. As he is doing this, I see—like every other spectator—the murderous
rope dangling out of the cassone and, like them, I wait for
Philip to notice it, too. But at nearly the same moment—in
this, *not* like every other spectator—I again catch sight of
the crooked candle on the cassone top; my brief (still lateral)

68

2.12 The candelabra has been turned around.

glimpse suffices to tell me that, since I last saw it, *it has been tampered with*. The candelabrum has been turned around, and the candle, formerly occupying the leftmost (or hindmost) branch, now stands in the rightmost (or foremost). By virtue of this reversal, the candle gives yet more scandal: it is now out of place in *two* ways (figure 2.12).

On this last provocation, I am hardly able to follow the story at all, though it is getting very busy, and this fact is no doubt what distracts other viewers from remarking the candle's reversed return. Philip sees the rope; Brandon yanks it out and lets in Mrs. Wilson, the housekeeper. As she chatters at Brandon in the foyer, Philip passes by with the tablecloth; together, the lovers lay the cloth on the cassone, which has been cleared for the purpose. Throughout all this, I seem not to breathe until Philip puts the candelabrum with the crooked candle back on the cassone. And to my great amazement after

2.13 Acceptable at last?

he does, the candle, now seen from a frontal angle, finally looks acceptable (figure 2.13)! More: with the candle again planted at the edge of the frame, the camera succumbs to the same back-and-forth tremor (the cinematic equivalent of Brandon's excited stutter?) that the candle had provoked earlier. The symmetry suggests an aesthetic whole; a sequence has been concluded, a chiasm rounded out, a "touch" laid on. My earlier despair proves merely an effect of my blindness to the operation of a classic fairy-tale logic of repetition and working through: the first correction must fail and likewise the second, but the third works the charm.

So my acumen comes into its reward; what felt like a pathology of viewing has been validated in an objective discovery. And I have found more than a minuscule aesthetic structuration; I have found a whole hidden level of Hitchcock's film-writing that, whether because its signs are too small, or too fleeting, or too peripheral, or too close to the obvious visual focus, we are ordinarily prevented from reading. I imagine how Jefferies must have felt in *Rear Window* (1954) when, wild with surmise, he got solid proof of Mrs. Thorwald's murder. But his elation is not what *I* feel; my discovery rather demoralizes me. For if the candle now looks right, this is only *more or less*. After what I've gone through, nothing in the film will ever again look just right; at most it will look "all right," passable. "Do you realize," Brandon reminds Philip just after the murder, "we've done it exactly as we planned, and not a single infinitesimal thing has gone wrong?" But my Hitchcock-issue monocle has brought me to a belvedere where such a view of things is no longer possible; infinitesimal things are always going wrong, even in a classically triadic narrative ceremony of righting them. I may have found the aesthetic, but it is not pretty: its processes work through to a correction that itself appears flawed, almost aggressively factitious.

And far from that prime motor of Hitchcockian narrative which is Murder, what I've discovered is an obscure little drama that will never matter to a narrative understanding of *Rope*, whether discovered or not. No wonder writers on *Rope* have subjected this drama, which surely some of them have also observed, to massive censorship.[4] Marginal to social, socializing content, it also tends to marginalize its observer, whose aesthetics would be too "precious" to have general value. Though my too-close attention proved an Open Sesame after all, what it sprung open was not a trove of recognizable treasure but a cabinet of curiosities whose use was anybody's guess and no one's concern. The candle is remarkably out of place but, unlike the windmill that turns against the wind in *Foreign Correspondent* (1940) or the nun wearing high heels in *The Lady Vanishes* (1938), it is not *importantly* out of place. In this, it contrasts with another droopy object in its vicinity: the piece of rope that Philip is horrified to see dangling from beneath the lid of the cassone. Were a guest to notice *this* oddity, it might be fatal to the perfect crime. But if the candle had been overlooked in the preparations, and a guest happened to observe it later, the only thing that would lose luster would be Brandon's reputation as someone who "always plans [his] parties so well." With the canting candle, Hitchcock employs one of his favorite forms (the "off" object), but empties it of its customary consequence; this candle sheds no other light but the obscure brilliance of its sly elaboration. This elaboration exemplifies what I call, in contradistinction to Hitchcock's recognized style, his secret style, a style that, like some faintly transmitted radio signal, can only reach those unhappy few who (by way of talent, pathology, luck, elective affinity) attend to the film too closely.

You would be right to think back to the hidden pictures of the preceding essay on *Strangers on a Train*, those microstructures concealed so deep in the film-text that they go unseen or, if they do happen to be remarked, cause the ostensible story to recede from view instead. But the bitty business around the canting candle does not just delineate another hidden picture. When Hitchcock hides a cameo or a charade, he is in no way *making a mistake*; these insertions purposely undermine narrative coherence. The candle framings, by contrast, crossbreed Brandon's narrative negligence with a mistake of Hitchcock's own, the kind known to film parlance as a continuity error. And in the very framing that finally puts matters "right," the candle is not the only object to flout continuity across the cut. Those sporting the monocle will have earlier observed that, in neatening a chair cushion

after David's murder, Brandon left a corner of it sticking up;
now, the unruly corner has been fastidiously turned down,
though no character in the film has had opportunity to ad-
just it. They will also notice a third item in need of adjust-
ment: Brandon and Philip have laid the cloth crooked. This
will be fixed later in the film, after the second hidden cut,
just as still later, after the third, the flowers that have been
attacked by Janet's napkin and Kenneth's elbow will find
themselves freshly arranged. There isn't the slightest narrative need for the ministrations of this phantom maid, and
her surreptitious housekeeping can hardly be likened to the
usual cleanup work of a "script girl."[5] On the contrary, all this
stealthy perfectionism generates secret *imperfections*. Crossing over from story to discourse, from enunciated to enunciation, correction becomes mistake; and in repairing Brandon's oversights, Hitchcock must resemble him in making
gaffes of his own, flawing the uninterrupted spatiotemporal
flow that is *Rope*'s obvious formal ideal. But with, as I'll be
showing, this crucial disparity: unlike Brandon, who never
notices his oversights (the cushion, the tablecloth, and even,
in the end, the candle), Hitchcock often seems complicit with
his own lapses, bestowing on them a strange, secret *assent*. If
Brandon's plan can't afford a single thing gone wrong, Hitchcock's seems to allow for plenty of them.

I call this strange allowance for error Hitchcock's *understyle*—by which term I mean to point up the double status
of so many of *Rope*'s continuity violations and technical
faults. These are presumably "below" the intentional threshold of both the recognized style and the secret style of the
hidden pictures; nonetheless, they enter into an inescap-
ably suggestive counterpoint with elements of style that *are*
programmed. If only in the eyes of the miserable elite who

penetrate to their recessed visibility, *Rope*'s continuity errors touch on a central aspect of Hitchcock's art; in disclosing an essentially faulty, clumsy, untidy Hitchcock, a Hitchcock who is endlessly making and cleaning up messes, and who seems to enjoy doing just that, they are instructively linked to the broader—and undeniably intentional—editing choices that the film is known for.

Imperfect Parfaits

The story of the perfect crime, I said earlier, is the story of the perfect crime's failure; let me now add that, normally, that failure never affects the story's form. On the contrary, it is precisely the crime's failure that allows the story-form to display the superiority of its own contrivance. The character whose mandate is to make a mistake is caught in a duel with the author whose equally mandated prescience is always exploiting the mistake to successful narrative effect. In this structurally unequal contest, the protagonist's not-quite-perfect crime proves the foil for the author's infallible perfect-crime story.[6]

What is different in *Rope* is Hitchcock's broad formal implication in his murderers' faultiness. As is well known, the film is a virtuoso display of cinema style; Hitchcock had the idea, he said, of doing it "in a single shot," but since this was not technically feasible in 1948, when the camera magazine held only ten minutes' worth of film, he did the next best thing, which was to film it in the longest takes possible: the eighty-minute feature has only eleven shots. But in opting for the long take, with its obvious technical limitations, Hitchcock must have confronted the inevitability of a certain number of false moves. The association of "take" with "mistake" and "mis-take" surely haunted him and everyone else on the stressed-out *Rope* set, where, as David Bordwell reminds us, "any missed cue or bungled line forced the whole production to start the shot over again."[7] The three main performances have retained an unacted nervousness that spikes through the script's overliterate finish. And even the characters' scripted mistakes have an odd way of being followed by Hitchcock's own continuity errors, as though the former, like a disease or a catchy tune, were contagious. If you're paying attention to the story, for instance, you notice that, just after Mrs. Atwater confuses David's friend Kenneth with David himself—and precisely on Brandon's words, "Uh, you've made a mistake"—Philip crunches his glass and cuts himself. If you're paying attention to the continuity, you observe that the wound has disappeared by the time Philip shows the astrologically gifted Mrs. Atwater his hands, and then, no less miraculously, is back again when he fights with Rupert over the gun.

But with *Rope*'s editing, Hitchcock has *systematically* integrated faultiness into the film's design. Though he said he wanted to do *Rope* in a single shot, much of his actual project involved an intricate treatment of the ten fault lines *between* shots where rolls were changed. Here is Eric Rohmer and Claude Chabrol's classic account of Hitchcock's solution to the problem:

> To maintain the sense of continuity, the interruptions due to the insertion of new film rolls in the camera were camouflaged. Half the time this was done by ending one roll and beginning the next with a close-up of the back of someone's jacket. The rest of the time it was done by picking up on glances, by cheating on the letter if not completely on

the spirit, since it is these latter splices that are least perceptible. . . . There was no other way. Hitchcock took into account
the fact that the projection reels are double the length of camera rolls. To pick up on the "back" of jackets would have required from the projectionists a precision that could not be
regularly counted on in practice. For this reason, every 600
meters—approximately, since the length of shot-sequences
is unequal—we have a classic reverse shot.[8]

For his two great French admirers, Hitchcock's gambit represents a technical challenge "won hands down." And yet it
is hard to see where the victory lies if, as they claim, the five
classic eyeline matches are *less* perceptible than the five vir-
tuosically hidden cuts.[9] On the contrary, the fact that the fault
lines in *Rope*'s continuity should become apparent just where
Hitchcock attempts to hide them suggests that the hidden
cuts, as such, are failures.

V. F. Perkins was perhaps the first to describe these failures
in close technical terms.[10] The first hidden cut, he observes,
"is spoiled by a sudden acceleration in the acting pace after
the join," the three following "by incomplete blacking out."
And though he deems the fifth and last cut "satisfactory,"
it too poses a pacing problem. However total, this blackout
is almost farcically short for the narrative moment: Rupert
closes the chest as soon as he gets it open, with time for only
a brief glimpse of the spectacle inside. But all such superfine
fault-finding may be unnecessary given awkwardness of a
grosser kind. Even lazy viewers must be given pause when
the camera, which has been gliding about the apartment im-
peded by no one and nothing, not even the walls, is suddenly
stymied by the irrelevant, but uncircumnavigable, back of
a man or chest. Or when the camera, foregoing its earlier

grace, pitches down and across this back in a baffling search for a blind spot. Or when the camera goes on to rack up *five* such fumbles over the course of the film. If you didn't know what Hitchcock was up to at these moments, you might think you were witnessing just plain bad camerawork. And even if you do know—that is, if you realize that these fits of gaucherie are so many feats of dexterity in *Rope*'s disorientated *tour de main*—you remain confused by the maladroitness of every brilliant hitch: never did virtuosity so suggest ungainliness. Rather than attempting to mask the cuts, Hitchcock seems, by masking them badly, to be arranging their display.

This counterassumption grounds the later reading of the cuts offered by Philippe Mather, an apparently more sophisticated reading than Perkins's, but one ultimately even more insistent on the cuts' failure.[11] Mather argues that Hitchcock's only way to get the audience to notice and appreciate his continuous camera "would be through the virtuosity of the hidden cuts, now recognized as not completely hidden." He proposes we think of the cuts as a set of classic special effects that "benefit from the simultaneous phenomenon of calling attention to the apparatus, or showing off, and justifying it through some form of narrative motivation." But having offered this appealing excuse for the cuts' poor concealment, he proceeds to find it not good enough. For one thing, what he calls their "fade to black" is a device that, over its long cinematic history, has tended to register an interruption of the film's temporality; when used here to promote continuity, therefore, it can only create "temporal confusion." For another, the narrative motivation of this device is "too weak"; there is no justification for, every twenty minutes or so, zeroing in on a back.[12] "It appears," Mather sniffily concludes, "that the hidden cuts in Hitchcock's film do not function as a remarkable special effect, and that they only risk being slightly annoying." If, for Perkins, the cuts failed simply by being visible, for the even more exigent Mather, they fail by being visible *in the wrong way*.

Despite the difference of approach—Perkins's technicism versus Mather's film semiotics—both critics are invested in the game of catching Hitchcock out, in compelling this reputed god to assume errant human form. As Mather's last sentence testifies, the game is not without a certain schadenfreude. Perkins himself admits that, though "the changeovers take up perhaps forty seconds of an eighty minute film," they are worth mentioning as "evidence against the conviction . . . that Hitch can do no wrong"; they "qualify, however minutely, the master's success in solving his chosen problem."[13] Both critics are obviously wearing a monocle, which they put to effective use; but their work is vitiated by the same contradiction: in harping on Hitchcock's mistakes, they uphold the flawless or code-obedient aesthetic norm that would be, or should have been, Hitchcock's ideal. What they fail to see is that their eyeglass is as much a part of Hitchcock's implicit organization of *Rope*'s viewing experience as 3-D spectacles are of *Dial M for Murder*'s.[14]

The visibly hidden cuts are not flaws to be discovered at Hitchcock's expense, behind *his* back as it were. Nor, forming with the manifest cuts an elegantly balanced system of ten, do they merely designate a historically unavoidable *technological* defeat that will be overcome in 2002 by the Steadicam of Alexander Sokurov's *Russian Ark*. Rather, they let Hitchcock acknowledge a fault that lies, primal and irreparable, at the core of his *art*. In each of them, he gives this fault three profoundly aesthetic forms. It appears, first, as a "designed" rupture in the aesthetic program (the *cut*); second, as the "beautiful" hiding of the rupture (the *masked* cut); and third, as the "witty" acknowledgment of the hiding (the *visible masked* cut). And though these forms of the fault—required, repaired, wryly self-aware—are dialectically linked, they do not appear in succession; each cut assumes all three forms simultaneously. That is why we hardly know how or why we are to perceive the cuts. This formal impaction is itself another sign—indeed, it is usually considered the sign par excellence—of artistic richness.

Let me now look at the third hidden cut, which, as Mather notes, is literally central, "situated halfway during the third projection reel, right in the middle of the film." Rupert is conveying into the living room a rather impressive if ambiguous pair of desserts: white molded concoctions each daubed with chocolate sauce and surmounted by a cherry; they are, one gathers, only miniaturized ice cream sundaes, but their conical tapering (no sign of individuated scoops here) suggests that they aspire to the smooth unbroken contours of a parfait or frozen mousse. En route, the teacher meets his star pupil, who has been quarreling with Janet:

> RUPERT: Something gone wrong, Brandon?
>
> BRANDON: No. Janet just has a talent for being bothersome at times. However, I suppose I'd better . . . *(turning back to Rupert)* uh, what did you mean, "something gone wrong"?
>
> RUPERT: Well, you always plan your parties so well, it's odd to have anything go wrong. She seems to be missing David. As a matter of fact, I'm beginning to miss him myself.

On the last line, the camera closes in on Brandon's back to effect the changeover.

Mather calls attention to the violation of spatial verisimilitude that occurs after the cut; Rupert is now standing on

2.14 The desserts before the cut.

the other side of the entrance, where Brandon had just been. "There has been a 100-degree shift in the diegetic space, and yet it goes by relatively unnoticed." Mather offers some possible reasons for our distraction (the alleged "temporal confusion" of the blackout, the "ongoing conversations"), but one he doesn't mention is the more striking continuity error involving the desserts themselves. For the two desserts Rupert is holding after the cut are not the ones he was carrying before it. On the right dessert, for example, the chocolate glaciers have become thin and runny, while the pound cake has doubled in thickness and lies on the other side of the mold (figures 2.14 and 2.15). In every main point of resemblance to its predecessor, this presque-parfait is far from perfect.

Here is a continuity error that, if not exactly committed on purpose by Hitchcock, he would certainly have known he couldn't avoid if he placed a hidden cut between the

2.15 The desserts after the cut.

desserts' presentation and their eating. These desserts are edible—else we should not see Rupert spooning one into his mouth after the cut; and by the time the following long take was set up—probably at least a day later—the originals would have been obviously unusable. To speak of originals at all is misleading; since each ten-minute take was filmed several times, there must have been a freezer's worth of replacements. *Rope*'s production conditions virtually mandate this fault; in no way could the desserts have been matched across a cut. And clustered around the fault is an exchange that, far from distracting us from it, seems to be alluding to it. "Something gone wrong . . . what did you mean, 'something gone wrong'? . . . it's odd to have anything go wrong." And I've been saving the cream for last. At the sight of the second pair of desserts, Mrs. Wilson exclaims: "*Two* desserts, Mr. Cadell?" The ambiguity that she can't possibly be aware of uttering (two desserts, two sets of two desserts), we can hardly escape hearing.

This odd level-jumping capacity is a frequent feature of *Rope*'s dialogue. "You don't think the party's a mistake?" captions the sight of the conspicuous imperfection that is the lopsided candle. Mrs. Wilson opines that "those candlesticks . . . don't belong there at all" just at the moment where the canting candle finally looks right. And just before the first hidden cut, Philip is demanding that Brandon find an "excuse" for moving the buffet to the cassone. "Why, we have a very simple excuse right here," Brandon replies as he reaches down to the pile of first editions on the floor. Whereupon, as if the word "excuse" had been suddenly summoned to double duty, the camera shifts to Brandon's back as proffering *Rope*'s own excuse for the screen's momentary blackout and the camera's concomitant roll change.

Apt, if not always accurate, these occult correspondences between the fiction and the filmmaking, between the dialogue of the one and the devices of the other, are "off" moments in their own right, maladroit metalepses. I am obviously not claiming that Hitchcock committed every continuity error in *Rope* with equal deliberation; but he hardly needed to. *Rope*'s understyle is so insistently organized around trouble spots— momentarily collapsed polarities of neat and sloppy, graceful and clumsy, clever and ruinous, continuous and fissured, meaningful and futile—that almost *any* continuity error may appear to be only another beguiling blot in the series.

Figures in the Carpet

What we call the Hitchcock Touch is an all-pervasive and unswerving style that links each image to every other.

This Touch is not a detail but a consistent general manner of treating all details; it is synonymous with Hitchcock's imposing will to totalization. With an insistence unique in the oeuvre, *Rope* invites us to see the great unifying Hitchcock Touch as a pointillism of discrete little touches; the single unbroken style scatters into the many mere details, as botched as they are brilliant, amassed in the understyle. If the Touch offers proof of a master, the touches never fail to announce their failure as slaves not just to technical circumstance but also to their own virtuosity—a failure registered sometimes as a fault within them, sometimes in the discord between them, and always in their collectively disharmonious relation to the whole. And given that Hitchcock disowned *Rope* for "breaking with" his usual filming techniques, the whole film may be considered just such a ruptive touch.

In this light, the film's formal climax comes in the long scene when the camera pans back and forth through the empty space of the apartment. "Suppose you were I," Brandon has just said to Rupert. "How would you get David out of the way?" As Rupert is offering his hypothesis, the camera moves to the vacant places where the events he imagines would have occurred. When Brandon would be letting David in, the camera crosses the living room to the hall, as if illustrating the action; when David would be given a drink, it lingers on the liquor table; when he would be asked to sit down, it shows us the armchair; and so on. This is the story's moment of truth. From Brandon's excitement, and Philip's despair, we know that what Rupert imagines comes close to what actually happened; he has successfully reconstructed the crime story, and what there is of mystery in *Rope* ends here. But with the camera apparently resigned to merely referencing his words, its movement should not be as compelling as it is. In pointing out the door, the closet, the chair, the piano, the camera seems to be doing more than just that, if we could only know what.

It is suggestive that, for most of Rupert's imagined narration, Hitchcock has depopulated the apartment; Rupert, Brandon, and Philip are nowhere to be seen, though the camera crosses past where they had just been standing. The apartment has become sheer "set." The emptiness brings out that quality of wastefulness which has always inhered in the leisurely—and, often enough, lumbering—movements of *Rope's* continuous camera. I find myself wondering why we must see, for instance, so much expanse of carpet? Then suddenly, my monocle focused on that carpet, I get it; I see track-prints, depressions, chalk marks—blemishes that could only have been caused during filming as equipment, walls, and furniture were being rolled away or repositioned (figures 2.16 and 2.17). The film isn't just "calling attention to the apparatus" with these marks; it is dirtying itself: Hitchcock's formal virtuosity literally streaks and spots the floor. Still supposing he is Brandon, Rupert continues: "I'd move quietly around behind the chair. . . ." And as the camera obediently moves around the chair, I discern yet another verbal-visual correspondence: Hitchcock *has moved the chair around.* He has evidently done so for the ease of the camera that now peers over that mussy/tidy cushion from above; and for the first time I observe a blackish stain on its seat (figure 2.18). Did David shit himself in the fright of being attacked? Or is it Rupert, the last to occupy that chair, who is responsible for its soiling? These are of course absurd conjectures; but at such a

2.16 Chalk marks.

2.17 Streaks.

2.18 Soiled seat cushion.

moment, to see the stain as merely a mottle produced by the
buckling of the brocade is equally naïve. It's more: it's the
signature of the artist.

The Most Unkindest Cut

Yet if, once again, Hitchcock haloes the Fault with an irony
that is tantamount to his admission and even aesthetic use
of it, what can be his purpose in producing so *many* such "signatures of the artist" in *Rope*? Or rather, why, despite their
number, do these signatures never seem quite enough? No
doubt, by virtue of this irony, owning an error becomes a way
of *becoming its owner*. As Roland Barthes says in *S/Z*, the function of classic irony is precisely to construct a wall of origin,
ownership, property.[15] If one looks for perfection in *Rope*,
the film will seem chockful of errors, but no sooner does

one attend to irony than—presto!—the errors will all seem
to vanish in a knowing wink. From this perspective, Hitchcock's understyle would do no more than extend a safety
net below the style's high-risk acrobatics; there every fault
or fall would be "caught" by the fine consciousness of an auteur who never nodded. And so the practice of irony-in-error
would regain the total, impregnable mastery that the practice
of perfectionism—at least in the eyes of those who don't miss
a missed trick—had to forego. Even the aesthetics of totality
would be repaired, as every instance of the film's imperfect
art stood revealed as an artful imperfection, a kind of beauty
mark that enhanced the features around it.[16]

Yet of the several reasons for doubting *Rope*'s dialectical
reunification by irony, the most convincing to you may perhaps be the fact that you will have already doubted many of
my examples of this irony. These must have been radically
uneven in their cogency; for every one you regarded as plausible or just possible, there was another you found outland-
ish or even delusional. "Understyle?" you surely thought to
yourself at more than one point. "Say, rather, overreading!"
But it is just this doubt about the pervasiveness of irony-in-
error that keeps the latter from being a *saving* irony: we can't
always be sure where it has or has not touched. As Barthes
again would say, the irony is not certain. And this uncertainty
lets us read the very practice of irony-in-error as a counter-
phobia that develops under the pressure—and possibly in
the very presence—of the unpredictable, unrecognized, and
unavoidable flaws it would ward off.

I illustrate the doubtful reach of this irony with a last con-
trasting pair of examples: two minuscule cuts near the end
of the film. With these cuts, a Too-Close Viewer is truly put
on his mettle (and risks appearing more touched than usual)

because, to my knowledge, *Rope* criticism has not only not identified them; it has dismissed a priori the very possibility of doing so. For, despite the common belief, confirmed in the most reputable quarters and repeated for convenience' sake here too, it is simply not true that *Rope* consists of only ten cuts: outside this decade, I have been able to locate two others.

The first supplementary cut comes soon after we see the blackened seat. Brandon interrupts Rupert's narration: "Then where would you put [David's dead body]?" "Well . . . ," but the camera, panning to the chest in anticipation of his words, shows Brandon moving toward it too and raising the gun in his pocket. Rupert, realizing his danger, changes his story midstream: "Well, I think I'd get Philip to help me carry him out of the room, down the back stairs." Still taking his words for commands, the camera occupies the axis of the empty hall that runs through the apartment's public rooms to the back door. The corridor is articulated, like classic Renaissance perspective, through a succession of decorative moldings at the entrance to each room; the door, which also has a molding, is further indented with small framelike panels. No less than with the tracking shot of tracks in *Strangers on a Train* or the cuts on cuts in *Psycho*'s shower scene, we are being asked to appreciate a piece of self-reflexive wit: this is a framing of frames (figure 2.19).[17] In all the literal and figurative archness, moreover, we may observe in the lintel beam of the outermost molding—the one closest to us—a central break between right and left halves. One could hardly ask for a better encapsulation of *Rope*'s formal tensions than this view of continuous space marked with a fissure.

And it is precisely on this image-emblem that a small jump cut occurs; right after it, Brandon steps into the center of the

2.19 Framing of frames.

frame, his head just under the lintel break, and stammers out, "Y-you'd be seen . . . y-you said yourself that if anything did happen, i-it must have happened in broad daylight." Once again, the technical fault (probably the price of facilitating the transition from empty to repopulated space) is not just technical; it exhibits the by now familiar coefficients of Hitchcock's aesthetic ironization. Not only is there the self-awareness around framing and fissures; the level-jumping dialogue vouchsafes even more self-awareness should the cut ever be seen—and be seen performed under studio lamps that, in Hitchcock's cinema, are always preferable to broad daylight. The cut may be all but impossible *to* see, but once it *is* seen, it shows the same patterns of error-management that we remark in the better visible examples.

The second supplementary cut is still harder to see, and by now that is saying a lot. It manifests itself as a tiny irregularity in the audio-visual synchronization of Rupert's final outburst to Brandon: "Did you think you were *God*, Brandon? Is that what you thought when you choked the life out of [David]? Is that what you thought when you served food from his *grave*?" Watch Rupert's mouth when he pronounces the words "his grave," and you will see a just-perceptible jump between the words "his" and "grave." But this cut—it just so happens, the last in the film—seems of a different kind from the other, from all the others. In the proper sense of the term, it should probably not be called a cut at all. It could not have been made during the filming since, with two actors onscreen, it would have been impossible to stop and resume shooting with so exact a frame match. Nor is it likely to have been a planned part of the editing; who would dream of cutting in the middle of a line of dialogue? Even with my monocle buffed to the utmost clarity, I see no self-awareness, no cinematic wit, no shadow of the author-in-charge. Elsewhere, I behold a complex art in the mistake, here only a simple mistake in the art: a postproduction tear mended with a splice.

Yet this glitch, alien to the *work*, is indisputably part of the *film*; visible in circulating prints as well as DVD and VHS editions, it cannot be an artifact of digital or video transfer. One might guess at half a dozen causes for the glitch—a reel dropped in the lab, a defective print, a flawed interpositive— without ever, at this date, hitting on the right one. But all such causes would have one thing in common: they would all be accidents befalling the film as a material technology, subject to the mishaps and degradations of physical things and to the malfunctions and breakdowns of mechanical equipment. *An infinitesimal thing has gone wrong*: a mistake that stands outside Hitchcock's practice of irony and would be, all unintentionally, the irony of that practice.

2.20 The neon cameo.

It is easy to imagine the Fault, as signature of the artist, carrying on the logic of Hitchcock's conventional cameo by other means: his fat body would be sublimated into an invisible "hand" whose nonetheless discernible "touch" vivifies his creation and identifies it as *his*. This speculative path is all the more inviting if we consider the slenderizing trajectory of *Rope*'s actual cameos. For there are two: the first, at the beginning, shows Hitchcock in flesh and blood walking down the street; the second, near the end, is a neon advertisement for a product called Reduco, in which Hitchcock is reduced indeed to the few line-strokes of his famous self-profile (figure 2.20).[18] But if we try to imagine the (unplanned, unwanted) glitch as a cameo, all that comes to mind is a corporeality that, no longer even the corpulent trademark of a majestic corpus, is as devoid of life as the corpse in the cassone. For in this moment, the work has *become* a corpse, gross, inert, an accident victim animated only by the material/mechanical contingencies of what is, in the aesthetic as well as physical sense, its decomposition.

And the Too-Close Viewer—what of him at such a moment? Personally, of course, he is caught up in the pathos of the catastrophe, which, though minor and momentary, must remind him of the death that he too harbors. But if this film-death is perturbing, it does not perturb him *more* than the proofs he has observed of the "living" film. After all, that he should find nothing (or find only something about which there is nothing to say) has been implicit from the outset in the "attention-surfeit disorder" that claims him, like Garrett Stewart's Poe, as its sufferer.[19] Whether this disorder enables him to discover an understyle undreamt of by normal spectators, or causes him to fall through that understyle's net into an abyss of insignificance, hardly matters to a practice that would be the same in any case. Neither success nor failure abates the hypertension of a scrutiny that is motivated less by a deliberate project of penetrating *Rope*'s secrets than by an involuntary compulsion to merge with *Rope*'s surface, to be bonded to it as closely as a lamination. The *project* can be (more or less) accomplished, but the *compulsion*, which repeats itself no matter what, is intractable; how could it be otherwise when it relies on a sense as ill-suited to the task as sight, which requires a distance from its object in order to perceive it at all? (The obverse of the too-close: the never-close-enough.) In his intimacy with Hitchcock's film, the Too-Close Viewer necessarily plays two roles: in one, he is its chosen confidant, to whom alone it whispers its closest secrets; in the other, he is its handpicked victim, whom it affects, like a disease, not only with its own notorious suspicion but also with that psycho-making vertigo against which the

suspicion feebly attempts to defend. At the end of *Vertigo* itself, Scottie can't stop looking—looking down from his tower
or, in the screenplay, looking out at the lights of San Francisco. Nothing, not even her death, drives away the drive to
Madeleine. Likewise, the Too-Close Viewer, though burning
his candle at both ends, cannot foresee not seeing forever, or
being at the end of his and Hitchcock's *Rope*.

The Long *Wrong Man*

And still I saw—but with such an exaggeration!

Poe

Soliloquy of a Spectator

Not long ago, in Paris (where such miracles still happen), I went to see a new print of Hitchcock's *The Wrong Man* (1956). It was doubly new to me, who had never before had a chance to see the film on celluloid. In the days before the screening, I primed myself for the revelation that theatrical projection would coax from this great work that I only knew in its debased condition as home entertainment. Already, in my mind's eye, I beheld the grain—the grandeur—the tremulous luminosity—of the bona fide cinematic images awaiting me. And in the event, I suffered no disappointment on this score: the chalky luster of Robert Burks's cinematography, formerly hidden from me in the brightness of the digital image, made the silver screen seem literally woven with silver. Yet if I had finally seen Burks's masterpiece, I perceived almost nothing of Hitchcock's. His great film, captivating, puzzling, distressing, and which I consider his most intense of all—here, this film seemed to be wearing a cloak of invisibility so ample that I half-suspected the so-called new print of being mutilated. Worse: in place of the masterpiece I anticipated, I saw a rather frigid little work—a bit dull, often sentimental—that I had never seen before and had scant interest in seeing again. After a while, I was able to identify this inferior work; it was, of course, *The Wrong Man* that I had read about in the critical literature: the film that Hitchcock asked Truffaut to file "among the indifferent Hitchcocks" and to which he claimed to be himself indifferent ("I don't feel all that strongly about it"); the film that Slavoj Žižek, voicing the opinion of many, proclaimed "leaves us cold"; the film in which Hitchcock is widely believed to have made the mistake of being true to life and hence false to his style.

What barbarism had perpetrated the replacement of that hugely compelling film I would watch at home by this mediocrity being projected under the same name at the Action Écoles? Only one thing: though the screen was now monumentally larger, the film itself was palpably shorter than anything I had ever watched on a monitor. It was not that, as I first thought, the copy being shown at the Action Écoles had curtailed the proper running time; rather, my home viewing practice had distended it, to a length that made this compact little film, when I finally saw it projected, virtually unrecognizable.

Never once, I was now obliged to own, did my home viewing of *The Wrong Man* come near coinciding with the running time of the Paris screening. Typically, it would extend through several days, sometimes to over a week; on a couple of occasions, it went so slowly that I gave it up in a sort of despair. Of the two main reasons for this lengthiness, one is the hyperattention that I habitually accord to *any* Hitchcock film, which I play most often at the tempo in music called larghissimo: very, very slowly. I do this because, in the normal procession of images in Hitchcock, I invariably have the frustrating sense of *a vision withheld.* It is as if there were always something crucial to be seen that somehow, whether through my lapse of attention or by the director's malice aforethought, has eluded me. At once demoralized and stimulated by the suspicion that I have missed out on this Secret, I find myself yielding to a desire to see more: more films, again and again, in greater detail. And no matter how *much* more the current state of technology lets me see, and yet how enigmatic the films remain, I persist in my absurd belief that I would understand them perfectly if only I could inspect them at greater length. It has been said, quite reasonably, that no *sane* person tries to enter the screen, but, with Hitchcock, that is precisely what I want to do: cross through the screen into the story world, to see, touch, possess the people and things there in a reality that, thus completely verified, would be hiding nothing.

Yet with *The Wrong Man,* I seem to harbor, in addition to this desire to see everything, its very opposite: an impulse to block everything out. In the grip of this impulse, closeness is no longer my eager ambition; it is, from the start, my painful condition. It is as if every frame secretly evinces the thing that eludes me in the other films, and, though I never can exactly state what this thing might be, it feels somehow monstrous—maddening—unbearable. I might say of this vision, as Judy in *Vertigo* says about the gray suit that fits her like a glove, and with the same emphasis: *I don't like it!* Straightaway, *The Wrong Man* makes me feel there is something wrong—wrong with *me!* What I see so disturbs me that, again and again, I turn away my eyes. Unsettled in my very person, I become subject to a hallucination far crazier than that of entering the screen: by a kind of reverse projection, *what's on the screen seems to be entering me*—and I am forced, by merely ocular means, to give intimate harbor to an obnoxious, but unrepellable, foreign body. In Hitchcock's less theatrical idiom, *The Wrong Man* "gets under my skin."[1]

Hence, the second reason why *The Wrong Man* takes me a long time to get through: the numerous and protracted breaks I take from watching it. These breaks have nothing to do with the various summonses—friends ringing, nature "calling"—that commonly extend home viewing time. Watching a Hitchcock, I am too devout to indulge such aesthetic irrelevancies for long—and in any case I should never think that I was *leaving* Hitchcock's world by going to objects so prominently featured in it as the telephone or the toilet. Still less do my interruptions have anything to do with the "longueurs" of this particular film. I am not sure I like *The Wrong Man*—I probably do not; I merely love it—but I am certainly never bored by it. Nor, finally, do these breaks offer merely well-deserved relief from the rigor of paying attention or the stress of bearing the unbearable. Far more aggressive than that, my breaks are inspired by a wish to actually break something: the film itself! With each interruption, as if the remote with its pause button were a revolver with its trigger, I shatter the filmic flow into amorphous pieces that will never, at least not by me, be reassembled. Attempting to save my own skin, I perforate the pellicle that is the image-continuum. After all, as Hitchcock himself acknowledged, the classic Hollywood film asks to be perused in a single sitting no less than the brief tale according to Poe.[2] And just as, for Poe, "simple cessation in reading" suffices to destroy the *tale's* "true unity," so the repeated adjournment of my viewing would disable the *film's* self-structuring as an aesthetic totality and diffuse its psychic effect as a single irresistible impression. Instead of Poe's taut short story, *The Wrong Man* would become a long loose novel that takes forever to finish and of which one is continually losing the thread. That may be the real domestication aimed at by my interminable home viewing: to *amortize* my distress over a long period of time, during which this overwhelming film would eventually become no more than another irksome but familiar household chore. And yet, to the extent I have succeeded, that chore remains as arduous as all a monk's austerities. Few things are more exhausting for me than watching a couple of minutes of *The Wrong Man*.

The following critical essay may be taken by the reader as a derivative of this soliloquy. In it, I will attempt to turn myself from an irresponsible spectator into a credible *speculator*: "one who engages in occult observations or studies" (*OED*), that is, a student of secrets. My purpose in becoming this speculator is not to renounce my long-established habits of fragmenting and protracting the film; the few excerpts under analysis are mere snippets, each lasting only a few seconds, and my reading will necessarily unfold at greater length than do its objects—even to the point of seeming to literalize the long-standing fantasy, running through textual criticism from Reuben Brower to Roland Barthes, of "reading in slow motion."[3] No, my purpose is to demonstrate that, for all its eccentricity, this long viewing sees a hidden truth in Hitchcock's film; specifically, that it lets us observe certain crucial little discords, minute but highly elaborated counterstructures, that are objectively present onscreen, but so well secreted there—by, among other things, normal projection speed—that they have never been recognized at all, much less accounted for. Consider my protracted viewing practice, then, as being akin to the secret vantage point necessary to discern the image in an anamorphosis. In other words, consider "The Long *Wrong Man*"—for so I call my interminable home movie with its extravagant hostility to formal unity—as a first, "hysterical" record of certain form-destroying discontinuities that, on reflection, can be shown to fracture *The Wrong Man* tout court. If I am persuasive in my speculation, the long film will have bespoken my intimate apprehension of the thing erratically pulsing through the short one: Hitchcock's secret style.

X Marks the Spot

With long, purposeful strides, Manny walks into the Victor Moore Arcade in Queens (12:39–50). He is bound for the office of the Associated Life Insurance Company, where he hopes to borrow money on his wife Rose's policy, but will instead be mistakenly identified as the man who held up the office a few weeks before. Though neither he nor the first-time viewer can know this yet, he is on his way to becoming the Wrong Man: behind him, his prudently overroutinized world of work and family; ahead of him, the disciplinary gulag of police, prison, and law court. The neorealist authenticity of a location shot does not quite conceal the mythic decor of a Portal. In approaching the infernal space of his ordeal, Manny must traverse a narrow, congested passageway; he is filmed from behind, denied all liminal affect, as though to suggest that he crosses this symbolic threshold without recognizing it as one. And just as, for Manny, this moment of transition would be only "dead time" between his intention and its realization, so, for most theatrical viewers, it is no more than descriptive filler interposed between important narrative articulations.

Yet this dead time, this filler, is marked by a slight but suggestive incident. As Manny enters the bottleneck of bodies, he seems about to bump into a man leaving from the opposite direction; in dress, at any rate (hat, gray overcoat, white shirt, black tie), this man is Manny's mirror image, a "front" that corresponds to the latter's "back." To obviate the run-in, the man cedes right-of-way, flattens his back against the wall of the passage, and sidles past Manny's shoulder. In crossing paths, each man has begun on the other's left and ends on his right, like figure skaters inscribing an elongated X on the screen surface. We cannot be sure whether they actually touch (like Bruno and Guy in *Strangers on a Train*) or just miss touching (like Guy and Hitchcock in the same film), but their auras, if not their bodies, have collided; and for one brief moment they are in each other's face. In acknowledgement of this awkward unexpected intimacy, the stranger flashes Manny a broad smile; and as if there were more to this intimacy than an accidental brush, the smile enigmatically lingers on his face, lapsing into a kind of satisfied grin, well after Manny has passed. When the crossover is complete, there emerges, in between Manny and the Lookalike (who now face in opposite directions), a pair of identically dressed sailors, whose faces, by contrast, are slightly turned toward one another (figure 3.1). And in a still denser patterning, just as we see Manny and the Lookalike begin this elaborate dance on the right side of the passageway, we also see another pair of pedestrians on the left side—a man and woman (neither of whom resembles Manny or each other)—complete *the same dance*. They too form an X pattern in passing one

3.1 Crossover complete.

another. Like Manny, the woman does not acknowledge her partner; he, however, like Manny's partner, acknowledges *her* with a long, full smile as he goes on his way. If their synchronization weren't a bit off, the couples would be performing in mirror symmetry (figure 3.2).

All of this happens in under three seconds. As an early iteration of the film's theme of the Double, the brief encounter does everything to make itself hardly visible. Most viewers pay it little attention because Hitchcock's quick, cluttered presentation obliges us to *skim* it, as nothing but a neorealist evocation of Manny's daily surround. Yet no sooner are we, by whatever means, brought to notice the incident, than, with a click—with a shock—it falls into place as a hidden picture of whose deliberate design we are perfectly convinced. The matched costumes, the chiastic ballet, the overlong smile— none of these details seems to us haphazard, let alone their confluence at this moment of transition. And the fact that the incident has been doubled by a banal version of itself— performed by anonymous characters who, far from looking

3.2 The two couples.

or dressing alike, are as normatively "different" as Woman
is to Man (whose appreciative smiles at her are anything but
enigmatic)—all this only increases, by antithesis, our sense
of signifying intent. We have been given something marked
"to be understood."

Is it possible for any self-respecting Hitchcockophile to
doubt what this thing is? Can such a one *not* recognize the
plot-initiating device that, as a signature formal structure,
has all the blatancy missing from it as a narrative event? No
question, we are assisting at an observance of the Transference. In this ceremonial (best known from *Strangers on a
Train*), two characters—one good, naïve, ordinary, the other
evil, conscious, an outsider—accidentally cross paths, and
the casual brush of bodies entails a fatal swapping of souls.
Desires, compulsions, crimes—all transmigrate between the
pair, so that the good character becomes afflicted with guilt,
while the bad one becomes the voice of conscience ("But,
Guy, it's *your* murder"). To identify the Transference in the
Arcade, then, is to know that, between the two men passing

one other, something else is being passed—namely, the culpability Manny is free of before the encounter that attaches to him right after. In brushing against Manny, the Lookalike would have foisted on him, like so much stolen money, furtiveness itself.

This instance of the Transference thrills me. For one thing, I see the titular theme germinating, feel the whole film, which has been tediously sentimental until now, starting to gel as an authentic Hitchcock text. But I don't simply recognize the Transference as a start-up device, like the footsie in *Strangers* or the confession in *I Confess*. I recognize it as a *hidden* start-up device, formed to frustrate optimum viewing, and disclosed only to the obsessive overzealousness of a viewer whom no amount of true-story rhetoric or location shooting can keep from looking more closely than he is asked to. My recognition thus attests to a passage of my own: I have crossed the *pons asinorum* of Hitchcockology—established my ability to prove the advanced, game-changing proposition (alas, so impossible for many to comprehend!) that Hitchcock's apparently hyperlegible art is a *secret* art, and as such often almost invisible. In confirming the astonishing ubiquity of Hitchcock's "hand," whose touches are laid on even the smallest cinematic particles, I simultaneously confirm my own intimate grasp of his style, in which the seemingly most negligible details are hiding esoteric forms.

And well might this understanding be under particular requisition in *The Wrong Man*. As everyone knows, the film is a reenactment of a famous story from real life: a case of mistaken identity in which a New York bass-player, Christopher Emmanuel Balestrero, was indicted for thefts committed by a man resembling him. In an opening address to the audience that is often said to substitute for his customary cameo,

Hitchcock even claims that "every word [of the film] is true." Though the statement is disingenuous (*and every image?* one wants to retort), Hitchcock does seem, quite designedly, to have renounced his usual stylistic implantation (suspense and the cameo), and even to have dispensed with artistic embellishments altogether, in favor of a rhetoric of plain speaking. He asked Burks to give him a "stark, colorless documentary treatment," and the filming was marked by a veritable fetishism of its real-life source: "action that took place at night had to be reenacted at night . . . in exactly the same way, in the very same spot"; "whenever possible, persons . . . who had figured in the story were hired to play their original roles"; and so on.[4] If Hitchcock here sounds like Visconti during the making of *La Terra Trema* (1948), no wonder; to depict this Italian-American reality, he wanted an American Italian neorealism, where the camera is made to disappear and "everything seems to be simply unfolding, as in life."[5]

But with the Arcade incident, he puts us in a position to know better—to know that his (familiar, manifest) style has not disappeared so much as gone into hiding. In this sense, the whole film promises to be one long hidden picture, in which we will find, under "natural" camouflage, the Hitchcock movie we thought we were being anomalously denied. Already, the air is humming with the same pleasurable purr as when, after *Vertigo's* long-winded exposition, Scottie sparks the engine of his DeSoto and starts pursuing Madeleine. The game is afoot, and those with eyes to see have left the True Story, which would never dare to claim a secret psychic transaction between Manny and the thief, for the Hitchcockian Fantastic, ruled by the constant presence of just that possibility.

With the familiar logic of the Transference as my basis, I

3.3 Reverse transference.

confidently make two predictions about what is to come in
the film. The first is that the Transference will be countered,
near the end of the film, with a Reverse Transference that
restores the exchanged psychic belongings to their rightful
owners (as in the half-struggle, half-embrace between Guy
and Bruno on the merry-go-round in *Strangers*, or between
Charlie and Uncle Charlie on the train in *Shadow of a Doubt*
[1943]). And indeed, *The Wrong Man*'s reverse transference
is unmissable (though unseen as such) by the most casual
viewer. I refer to the famous "miracle" shot in which, apparently in answer to Manny's prayers, his face gradually
changes into that of the Right Man, whom the camera proceeds to follow on the robbery that finally establishes him
as the real thief (figure 3.3). Once again, during the brief lap
of the dissolve, each man is in the other's face; but now the
chiasm first enacted as a barely visible narrative incident, a
chance crossover of two characters, is reversed by a bravura
camera effect that thus doubly earns its name as a cross fade.
In it, the identities blurred in the Arcade get sorted out, with

the culpability wrongly attributed to Manny repinned on the rightful robber.

My second prediction is that, in the finally disclosed Right Man, I will recognize the enigmatically smiling Lookalike in the Arcade, who, also in the manner of a hidden picture, had been there right in front of our eyes as early as, for Manny, the unlucky-thirteenth minute of the movie. Yet here I am sorely disappointed. Certainly, the resemblance of these two men is striking—much more striking than the resemblance of either to Manny—and one critic, without even seeing the Transference, has claimed to find what its logic tells me should be there. According to Marshall Deutelbaum, the Lookalike is none other than the actor who plays the Right Man (Richard Robbins). But when I compare the two, it is apparent right away that the Lookalike has thicker features and higher eyebrows; his sideburns are different in both shape and proximity to the ear; and, if the cut of his coat is similar, the cloth is certainly not. There is no doubt in my mind: the Lookalike is *the wrong Right Man* (figure 3.4).[6]

And yet the near resemblance between the Lookalike and the Right Man seems as much the result of deliberate planning as the Arcade incident. Even after we have established that the Lookalike is not the Right Man, the crux remains crucial. It would be a far grosser error than Deutelbaum's to believe that nothing is going on in the Arcade but a film realism by whose tenets people in crowded passageways are "naturally" at risk of colliding. From consulting production and camera reports, Bill Krohn has learned that Richard Robbins was not present on the set when the Arcade scene was being shot; and he reinforces this archival finding (which has no more probative value than any other attendance sheet) with an appeal to plausibility that dismisses a lot more than

3.4 The wrongish right man.

Deutelbaum's misidentification: "While Hitchcock could be Nabokovian, in this film, he was so determined to hew to the facts he told Truffaut he regretted having imposed any dramatic shape at all."[7] This too seems wrong to me, both in the logic whereby Hitchcock's resolve to hew to the facts is considered supported by his regret at *not* having done so, and in the overall refusal to recognize the film's proliferation of doubles and crossovers, which I should think is nothing if *not* Nabokovian.

If Deutelbaum were right, the Arcade incident would be the support of a "strong" structure of meaning; if Krohn were right, it would inaugurate no signifying process whatsoever. The truth seems to lie—dismally—in between. Neither full

nor empty, the Transference is only exasperatingly defective. It is not absent, but as a presence, it lacks sufficiency; a
radically "spotty" form, it falls short on follow-through—on
continuity. Imagine a game of dot-to-dot in which, by error or
diabolical arrangement, some dots have been misnumbered,
and some are missing, while the majority remain in proper
sequence. When you compliantly finish the puzzle as per instructions, you will simultaneously confront (1) the object as
it ideally *should be*; (2) the object as it really *is*, slightly but
insistently "off"; and (3) the maddening duplicity of an object
that is both right and wrong at once. So it is with Hitchcock's
misconnected images of the Transference; it is not obvious
how, or even if, one should proceed to put them to rights.

I do not find Hitchcock's recognized style intact, then,
once I have penetrated its drab neorealist incognito; instead,
I am brought to face a stylistic *inconsistency* in which the director, by means of the most meager signage, has given me
an identity that, with the same minimalism, he proceeds
to take away, doubling or dividing it. In my difficulty, I am
like Iris in *The Lady Vanishes* when she is told that Miss Froy,
who is missing, has never existed, or when later, by a reverse
deception, she is shown a lady in Miss Froy's clothes who is
nonetheless not Miss Froy; I too do not feel completely right
in the head. "Do I see what I think I see, what the others say
isn't there?" And unlike Iris's persistence, my own gets me
nowhere; as the upshot of my labors, I reach a dead end,
as though the ultimate confirmation of my intimacy with
Hitchcock's style could only be this interpretative futility.
The many X's marking the Arcade incident—more, even,
than I've mentioned[8]—might as well be variables in algebra,
values constitutively unknown. And if it is bad enough to
know that something is *being* meant while nothing, finally,

is meant, it is worse to understand that, in coming to know so much and no more, I am myself the living support and habitation of this enigma, which hardly exists except in my too-close relation with a style whose "secret" seems to be keeping *me*. It is thanks to such deviously involving games that the phenomenology of my viewing realizes Hitchcock's well-known ambition to abolish the fourth wall—or what *Stage Fright* (1950) calls the safety curtain—of cinematic illusion. Here that wall has disappeared under—and even by means of—my very eyes, whose overattentiveness to the Hitchcockian Transference handpicks me to be its offscreen object. I naturally protest: "I don't like it!" But only to hear back: *it fits you like a glove!*

Getting Things Wrong

Having come so far, though, I realize that I have just re-enacted, as my own viewing experience, the double movement of *The Wrong Man*'s very story. Just as that story contrived that Manny and the thief should be first confused, then disambiguated, so too, this faint collation of hidden pictures invited me initially to presume, and finally to repudiate, the Lookalike's identification as the thief. Miraculously, the misalignment of the sign has become a sign of misalignment, and as such, may be seen as having a lesson to teach us: to think twice—as Manny's accusers should have done, and Deutelbaum too—before positively identifying anything! In pursuing my undermotivated, overinvested meanderings across the film's visual field, then, I seem to have been unknowingly practicing a scrupulous forensics. Hitchcock has set me a sly test, to see if I can tell the difference between two men who look alike. And in this story of error-based injustice, having got a thing right, I have implicitly *done the right thing*. I become the spectatorial avatar of Police Detective Matthews, the film's eventual Good Cop who, having observed the resemblance between Manny and a thief just caught in the act, concomitantly grasps the implications of the fact that it can be no *more* than a resemblance.[9]

Yet it would be wrong to celebrate my unexpected reenactment of the story as a sort of morality of "right seeing" shared by the auteur with his hyperattentive viewer.[10] Such a morality would presuppose that the screen image is itself correct—that we only need to scrutinize it carefully to get at the truth of things. But it is not merely hysterical secretaries, smarmy cops, or overconfident observers like Deutelbaum, who, in the name of likeness or likelihood, make visual mistakes in *The Wrong Man*. Hitchcock himself makes them in the film's numerous continuity errors. Were I to count these errors, *The Wrong Man* would perhaps have no greater share of them than any other Hitchcock film, but it is here that I notice them most readily and in greatest profusion. Far from requiring me to slip on my monocle, they stand bare before my naked eye, brazenly demanding the recognition from which I normally suppose they shyly withdraw. Of what camouflage—what decency—have they been stripped?

Few viewers, after all, see continuity errors when Alicia is stealing Sebastian's key in *Notorious* (1946), or Bruno is attempting to retrieve the lighter (although such errors demonstrably exist). We have a habit of calling the suspense of these sequences "unbearable," but it is actually just the opposite: we bear up under it quite well; in publicity lingo, it *holds* us like nothing else. Suspense is the binding agent of Hitchcock's cinema, overlaying the image-continuum with the additional continuity provided by a gripping story;

it cements us to the images, and the images to one another. But this binding is blinding. In suspense's grip, we consume every image with burning impatience for the next, and the one after that; *all* the images strike us as so many obstacles standing in the way of the outcome that, by deferring it, and then deferring it again, they make us anticipate more eagerly than ever. And thus addicted to the image flow, our attention to any *one* image is not likely to be very keen.

Hitchcock as good as tells us in his opening address, however, that this formative element of suspense is missing from *The Wrong Man*.[11] The film has no Albert Hall, no Prairie Stop or flight from Phoenix, and in the lack of such sequences, it loses, if not its plot, any plot it can coax us into caring about. Between the diabolical transference that inculpates Manny and the miraculous reverse transference that exonerates him is only a thin string of incidents that refuse to "build." If this spectacularly fitful story dramatizes anything, it is its own repeated failure to accrue momentum. Looking for three witnesses, Manny finds two already deceased and, along with the script and most viewers, forgets the third—that third which is, as Peter Brooks has noted, the minimum increment for narrative. If in plot-driven films, we forget particular images, in this one we can hardly recall the story line![12]

Not only drained of suspense, then, but also disenthralled from a plot too weak to hold the stage, the image in *The Wrong Man* acquires a uniquely raw, refractory aspect. Foreground and background, essential narrative articulation and contingent filler—these normal polarities of vision are so enfeebled that the entire visual field often looks like an unsortable blur between them. In other Hitchcock films, we are given precise instructions—now verbal (a character's remark), now visual (the camera's framing)—on where to look; the image is essentially read for us.[13] But in the black-and-white *Red Desert* (1964) that is *The Wrong Man*, the image lacks its usual strong dose of this pregiven purposefulness. It offers us its visuality—its ocular provocation *as* image—with an opacity never before known to the Master of Suspense. (How often in the film do we find ourselves literally staring at the wall!) My attention is initially *baffled*, uncertain what it should heed; then, it becomes *hyperactive*, by quick turns farsighted, myopic, direct, oblique, rapid, patient, whatever might make the image yield (yield enough, at least, to make all this busyness worthwhile); and finally, it gets *tired*, sufficiently relaxed to be at the disposal of curiosity, obsession, reverie, a stroke of luck. In short, I find almost nothing to do with the image except, now one way, now another, *look at it*.

Almost nothing: I see something wrong with it. "But that painting wasn't there before! Weird, the cup has changed places! Look, that's a different number on the van!" Curiously, in my suspense-deprived state, I find myself reproducing suspense's own initiatory figure: "Listen, did you notice anything wrong about that nun?" "That's funny, they're dustin' crops where there ain't no crops!" "But it *isn't* dark, Annie, it's a full moon!" Hitchcockian suspense begins precisely when someone observes that *there is something wrong in what is seen*: a tiny anomaly in the natural or conventional order of things that Pascal Bonitzer, following Lacan, has termed "the stain."[14] In detecting the narrative-cinema norm (what we call "continuity") as slightly but unmistakably spoiled by the thing-that's-not-right (what we call the "continuity error"), I too become an Observer-of-the-Stain. So much again for the fourth wall, always collapsing under—and through—my eyes!

But when the task of looking for the Stain is thus taken

offscreen and thrust upon me, it changes character. In one essential respect, of course, the continuity error should be the exact opposite of the stain. Whereas the stain, verified by characters and viewers alike, has utmost pertinence to the fiction, the error, observed, if at all, in silence and solitude, seems to have none; and while the meaning of the stain goes (humanly) deep, the scant explanation deemed necessary for the error stays on the (no more than technical) surface. "It's only that" there wasn't enough cover footage; the sequences were shot at different times; someone goofed. Accordingly, nothing is *less* interpretatively exigent than a continuity error, whose meaning is at once fictionally null and technically trivial. It enters our vision as what we *shouldn't have seen* and what (provided we don't have to do this often) we promptly cordon off from our understanding to preserve our pleasure in the film's coherence. Yet even to perform this quasi-automatic segregation presupposes a prior moment in which we have taken the error for an integral part of the fiction. Even to think "Something's wrong with this picture," we must have grasped the picture as an organized whole, a gestalt; and we can only say "But that doesn't make sense!" because for a baffled moment we'd assumed it did.

It is this baffled moment that, in watching *The Wrong Man*, I never manage to get beyond; wherever I notice a gaffe, I can't help noticing its odd *aptness*. The film's numerous continuity errors seem to lead a double life. On the one hand, they imply things impossible in the true story that Hitchcock is filming; on the other, they prove curiously well-suited to the hidden picture that he is filming on the *pretext* of that story. They are alternately mistakes without meaning and meanings in the mode of mistake. The authorial intention standing behind such errors is, of course, hugely variable. Sometimes Hitchcock seems to have merely acquiesced in these tiny flaws as the inevitable consequence of the vagaries of editing, shooting schedules, budgets, and human nature. At other times, he seems to have gone out of his way to manufacture such flaws, as if they were not flaws at all, but subtle touches favorable, even necessary, to his art. And much of the time, it is difficult to distinguish these two forms of error-production—to know if Hitchcock is *letting* continuity errors happen, nonchalantly assuming that, barely visible, they will pass undetected, or if he is *making* them happen, secretly hoping, with these barely visible, but repeatedly seen, phenomena, to form a sort of thin ice through which even a mass audience might find itself suddenly plunged into the chill intimacy of "too-closeness."

We've seen how, in *Rope*, Hitchcock's mistakes—mistakes inherent in the project of a one-shot film—found ironic acknowledgment in the story of the "perfect crime," where characters often seemed to be unwittingly alluding to them.[15] What I called the understyle was an interpretative zone organized in the interface between story and filmmaking, where cinema's so-called master allowed even the unmastered to grip us—and turn to a sense of meaningfulness. In *The Wrong Man*, too, human error is the very subject of the story, and here it is not an individual but a collective failing for which a whole disciplinary network is to blame. What is Manny, after all, but the tragic personification of a continuity institutionally presumed where none in fact exists ("The man at the window is the one that's been here before")? This thematization of "wrongness" shines ultraviolet light over otherwise invisible ink; it lets us read, rather than repudiate, the continuity errors as a *systemic* feature of Hitchcock's film-writing, in which they forge so many links between a wronged man and a flawed cinema.

From the overwhelmingly vast field of errors in *The Wrong Man*, let me propose a pair of examples that illustrate the poles of its organization:

1. *The Moving Cup (5:24–41).* Coffee in one hand and newspaper in the other, Manny is about to occupy an empty table in Bickford's. After a nondescript side view of Manny approaching the table, we get the best possible view of the cup he sets atop it (figure 3.5). Classically ensconced in a matching saucer, the cup is placed so that its handle juts out at a right angle and we can read the Bickford's name emblazoned on its side. But when the camera then cuts to a head-on view of Manny sitting down, the cup, like a diva who insists on being photographed from her most flattering angle, remains "facing" us in exactly the same way (figures 3.6 and 3.7). To retain this ideal orientation vis-à-vis the viewer, it has had to change its actual orientation relative to Manny. With no apparent way of doing so, *the cup has moved* (along with the clump of sugar, salt, and pepper shakers, which otherwise would now be obstructing our view). And this is not the only time in the scene when the saucer behaves like a baby model of the flying kind. Settled at last into his chair, Manny retrieves a pencil from his coat and prepares to annotate the racing schedule; with his free hand, he reaches to pick up his cup of coffee. The camera cuts to a close-up of the racing form, on which Manny has just begun making notes; the cup is visible only as the dark shadow it casts alongside the newspaper—and has not cast before (figure 3.8). Again, so little time has passed from the previous shot that the audio track carries over, unbroken, the

3.5 Cup, take 1.

3.6 Cup, take 2.

sound of a siren—and yet the shadow confirms that *the cup
has moved a second time* with Manny's hand nowhere near it.

These miniscule discontinuities are hardly the result of
novitial ineptness. Plainly, the coffee cup has been moved in
the first instance so as to keep its ideal form (handle on the
right, the Bickford's name full on).[16] It must keep this form not
simply because it looks better that way, but also, less simply,
to maintain the iconic simplicity of the overall framing—call

3.7 Cup, take 2 continued.

3.8 Cup, take 3.

it "Still Life of Man with Coffee Cup and Newspaper"—being developed to convey the unchanging character of Manny's after-work routine. Likewise, the cup's shadow, ominously inverted, is more evocative than if, in strict continuity, Manny's hand were muddling it. Far from failing to spot and correct such "errors," Hitchcock has deliberately engineered them. Such liberties stand at the heart of his compositional practice, in which important objects are consistently framed

THE LONG WRONG MAN / 117

to look like Platonic ideas of themselves—not a key, but quintessence of Key, not a tower, but Turricity itself. Such beautifully archetypal clarity never fails to trump a realism in which a cup, for example, would never suddenly swivel around, the better for us to appreciate its Cupness. In the light of this manifest aesthetic destiny, it seems wrong to call the moving cup a flaw at all; art has negated our very perception of error.

2. *The Phantom Van.* After a night in the 110th Precinct police station in Queens, Manny is herded into a police van, which is then seen driving him across the Queensboro Bridge to Manhattan, first to Police Headquarters and later to Felony Court. The van in figure 3.9 is plainly numbered 1437 in three places, but the van in figure 3.10, a single cut later, flashes us a no less visible 1403 in the same three places. Then in figure 3.11, several cuts later, the van number has changed back into 1437. Technicist common sense readily explains how this embarrassing slipup must have happened: the shots with Van #1437, both requiring Henry Fonda's presence, were most likely filmed back to back; the long shot showing Van #1403 in transit, for which the actor's presence was not necessary, was taken at another time, by a second crew, and with a different van. In the course of production, some hapless assistant—perhaps even the second unit director himself— got a number wrong, and that is all. Nothing mitigates the blatancy of a classic continuity error in full, unfragrant bloom; error has negated all sense of art.

Now, in first choosing these examples, I meant them to establish an opposition between the mistake that isn't one and the mistake that is, between error as art and error as error. And yet the more I contemplated them, the less satisfactorily

3.9 Van A.

3.10 Van B.

they seemed to do the schematizing work I'd assigned. After all, even with the moving cup, we don't just behold the serene lucidity of a "beautiful composition"; we also see evidence of the unnatural agitation by which that composition comes to be made—and in due course unmade. The cup's hyper-realist precision within certain frames comes at the cost of the untenable, slightly maddening discontinuities between

3.11 Van A again.

them. Under these incompatible twin aspects, the cup is both ideally cuplike and continually out of sync with itself.

The whole field of inanimate objects in *The Wrong Man* teems with a similar duplicity, once you train your eyes to see it. Bottles, placards, doors, cars, and God knows what else emerge into compositional focus out of a peripheral turmoil in which, between cuts, they change position, morph into one another, appear from nowhere, or disappear as if they had never existed, even though all such shifts should be ruled out by the real-world laws governing the story. And in this mass defection of "dots" from their prescribed connection, most of the objects do not have even the cup's vocation; they are never called to center stage, but remain in a background that is nonetheless, between the joints, forever jumping. The problematic of the moving cup is thus writ large all over the film in the tension between Hitchcock's signature clarity and this underlying visual static that is constantly disturbing it. "Does Hitchcock intend this static?" What is certain is that he doesn't in the least resist it, that this is a domain his perfectionism has chosen not to colonize. It is a continuing logical interference in the system about which we can only say for sure that his art *superintends it*. And yet if the static does any remotely aesthetic work at all, it is only *to rupture the aesthetic*—the hyperlegible, super-suspenseful "holding environment" that is Hitchcock's signature style. This results in a crazy-making atmosphere in which every object in the films appears both as itself and as a psychic projection—of whom or what one usually cannot even say.

And the Phantom Van? Just as the beautiful composition necessitated "ugly" continuity errors as its condition of possibility, so, conversely, the nonpertinent van error enjoys a surprisingly strict relevance to the main argument of Hitchcock's cinema. At first sight, of course, the error shocks me, and far more than if it had been made by another director. "Oh, the irony!" I can't help exclaiming: the irony, first, that Hitchcock, famous for his scrupulous advance planning, should commit a continuity error this obvious, let alone in a story obsessively concerned with being true to life; the irony, second, that the source of error should be, of all things, a number, when his camera typically pays such meticulous attention to numbers as to be frankly fetishistic;[17] and the irony, third, that the breach in continuity should occur in a shot whose only reason for being is, precisely, to *insure* continuity: a classic "bridging shot" of the van literally crossing a bridge from Queens to Manhattan.[18] Eluding so many checkpoints, the misnumbered van irrupts into my field of vision almost traumatically, as the catastrophe that every precaution has been taken to avoid. But, I realize, it thus replicates the logic underlying Hitchcockian narrative itself. This is the logic most lucidly expressed in *Vertigo* when Madeleine says to

Scottie, "It wasn't supposed to happen this way," to which he retorts, "It had to happen." This is also the logic by which, in *The Wrong Man* in particular, trouble comes to Manny "even though"—that is, for the very reason that—he has arranged his life to avoid getting into trouble. The Phantom Van would stand at the antipodes of Hitchcock's art, if the latter weren't an art that rigorously destines everyone and everything to reach just such an opposing point of self-contradiction. This error may not be logically consistent within the story, but it *is* an inevitable product of the universe of misrecognitions and false continuities of which that story is itself another inevitable product. As such, it belongs to, and has even in a manner been predicted by, the author who proves no less subject to his cinematic worldview than anyone else.

More: no small part of the awkwardness of the correct/incorrect/corrected van pattern (reminiscent of the canting candle in *Rope*) is that it makes for a rather silly narrative rhyme with Manny's own tripartite ordeal—even literally, for who can contemplate this error for half a minute without these words coming unbidden to mind: "They got the wrong van!" The wit is so inevitable as to seem hard-wired into the error itself; and given Hitchcock's subterranean insistence on the absurdist pictographic puns I've called his charades,[19] it is just possible that what we took for an unfortunate mishap was designed by him for the sake of a joke that couples the soulful story world with merely mechanical filmmaking as odd variants of one another. I can't prove this proposition as a fact, but no one can escape it as a conjecture. Hitchcock's understyle—the strange dialogue he insinuates between story and storytelling technique—is always giving rise to just such equivocations between intention and inattention, mastery and mistake, the art of error and the errors of art.

Most distinctively, then, Hitchcockian Error does not happen purely "on purpose," in sharp contrast to the many unplanned errors around it; nor does it happen sheerly "by accident," independent of all design; it happens, as children like to say, *accidentally on purpose*, in a cross-breed of artfulness and error so stubbornly insistent on both its terms that neither ever succeeds in annihilating the other. Here, error seems essential to what Hitchcock's art wants to say *but can say in no other way than by lapsing from lifelikeness*. Accordingly, I offer a second pair of examples in which the error involves nothing less than the canonical figure for lifelike representation: the mirror.

3. The Vanishing Mirror. Near the beginning of the film, when Manny comes home from work, milk bottles in hand, we see a large oval mirror hanging in the hallway (figure 3.12; 5:59–6:08). A day later, when Rose makes a phone call in the same hallway (figure 3.13; 28:01), the mirror has disappeared, its place taken by an imitation Turner seascape. The mirror remains absent in two subsequent hallway scenes: when Manny's brother-in-law also makes a call there (43:44–45:18), and when Manny and Rose return home and are greeted by his mother and their sons (56:26-47). But near the end of the film, Manny is again shown returning home from work, milk bottles in hand once more, and the mirror has reappeared in its former place (figure 3.14; 1:14:50–15:03).

The continuity offense is flagrant, but technicist common sense is less helpful than with the wrong van. No doubt, the two Manny entrances, which look practically identical, were filmed at the same time, as perhaps were the two other hallway scenes; but why would the mirror be removed from the other scenes, when the statuette, lamp, and two side tables

3.12 Hall mirror.

3.13 Hall mirror gone.

3.14 Hall mirror back again.

have been retained? No doubt, when one person, or several, stood near the mirror, it was difficult for the camera to avoid being seen in reflection; but in that case, a curious insistence must attach to putting a mirror on the wall in the first place. Certainly, when the mirror does appear, it dominates the composition; on Manny's right as we follow him entering, it reflects the inner staircase on his left—a fact which, far from opening up the space in the way decorators recommend, only makes it more confining; and this creepy doubling function is itself creepily doubled: before we see Manny in the mirror, we see his shadow cross the wall it hangs on. It is improbable that, with so strong an accent, this prop was simply forgotten in the scenes where it is absent; far more likely, it was purposely deselected. Yet if the disappearing-and-reappearing mirror makes for an obvious narrative gaffe, it also lays down, in the very guise of gaffe, an important, otherwise unutterable counternarrative truth. Why, after all, may the mirror appear only when Manny is alone in the hallway? Why, if anyone else stands there, or even stands there *with* him, must it disappear? This mirror, evidently, is no ordinary realist object; it is Manny's familiar, disclosed in his solitude as the emblem of some uncontrollable psychic power that operates in or near him. By contrast to *Psycho*, where every character is sooner or later seen in a mirror, in *The Wrong Man*, where we observe several mirrors besides this one, no one but Manny is ever seen reflected in any of them.[20]

I take the erroneous mirror to be doing the (sly, tentative) work of transposing Manny from realism to the fantastic. If Manny were a creature in 1950s Japanese sci-fi, we might call him the Human Mirror: "wherever he goes, he makes doubles of himself!" Sometimes this cloning capacity results in a physical resemblance (not only the Right Man, but also the whole multitude of facsimiles who spring up around Manny); sometimes it facilitates psychic projection (Rose acts out his incipient madness, and even, in a curiously amateurish—or unguardedly loving—shot of Manny in prison, the camera replicates his dizziness as its own dizzied view of him). This man who, in everything but height, is the little man par excellence, serves as the operational field of formidable occult forces; to trigger Manny's replication, his presence is, one way or another, always required. (Proof *a contrario*: when, worried about Manny's absence, Rose calls the hospitals, she finds that "they didn't have anyone answering his description"!) Unlike the telekinetic Carrie twenty years later, though, the specular Manny exercises his powers without rhyme or reason, intention or desire. He is less the agent than the arbitrarily designated node of a Transference gone wild. The creatures created in the wake of this Human Mirror are always a bit off, imperfect copies about whom one is never sure just how much of Manny they will replicate. Manny is not a thief, not a black man, a woman, a camera, or Hitchcock; yet sooner or later each of these many Mannys, all of whom are the wrong Mannys, will be summoned onscreen in his vicinity to double some one of his facets: his appearance, his socially presumed guilt, his paranoia, his vertigo, his misrecognition. Like the Arcade transference, the mirror error introduces into the film's realist prose an insane, barely whispered poetry. It is a kind of closet from within which Hitchcock advances the claim that average-appearing Manny is *paranormal*, a claim that, as a true-story proposition, is so obviously unconvincing, irresponsible, and even offensive that it can be admitted only surreptitiously, as a

3.15 Cracked.

cinematic lapse. In this strategy, Hitchcock hides the poetry under realist décor, which in turn, however, he strains to the breaking point.

4. The Crazy Mirror. It is no accident, then, that the film's nightmare of contingent doubling and unstable self-projection reaches its apogee when a mirror literally does fracture. I have in mind the extremely brief, but all the more memorable, shot in which we see Manny's wounded forehead through a cracked mirror after both have come under assault by Rose's hairbrush (figure 3.15). The wound not only literalizes the "bad breaks" that his mother, euphemizing the vulnerabilities of a whole class condition, blames for Manny's troubles; it also literalizes the psychic fault lines in the adamantly regular persona that Manny (whose imagination of disaster is no less well-developed than his paranoid wife's) maintains as a means to cope with that condition. If this startling shot seems uncannily familiar, a making explicit of what was, charade-wise, already there, that is

3.16 Wire throttling Manny's head.

3.17 Manny's face cloven by bar shadow.

because, throughout the film's visual treatment of Manny, there is always something amiss with the image of his head. Though the head itself is well shaped, an unsightly, vaguely menacing detail often spoils its periphery, now a spikelike column just above the skull, now an electrical cord ready to throttle the neck (figure 3.16). Sometimes, the head is bisected by the shadow of a prison bar, say, or a hanging microphone at the police station (figures 3.17 and 3.18). Even his

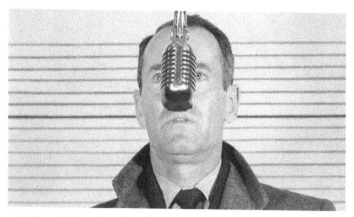

3.18 Manny's face cloven by mike.

3.19 Stain on crown of Manny's hat.

unflattering, but ubiquitous, hat does its part to make Manny look "wrong in the head," with a small stain on the crown suggestive of seepage (figure 3.19).[21] The cracked mirror is the culminating disfiguration; it is as though the face itself, and not merely the mirror, had cracked in half and its two parts could never be realigned. "You're not so perfect," Rose has just told him; in disclosing what Renata Salecl derisively calls "the cracked, clownish face of an obscene madman," the mirror compels us to see Rose's own breakdown as an acting-out of the breakdown that Manny—here, the Human Mirror in excelsis—has been doing everything *not* to have.[22]

And these are not the only splits this famous shot registers—or rather, Manny is not the only register of its splits. The camera's own framing has taken the place of the mirror's so that the crack cleaves through the image as if the lens, too, had been fissured by Rose's violent brush.[23] And that seems right, because the image, like Manny in it, is all wrong. Accidentally on purpose, it explodes with more continuity errors than can be conveniently counted. I observe, first, that Manny stands taller than the top of the mirror; second, that he is not looking at the mirror when he is struck, but at Rose alongside it; and third, that her blow causes his head to jerk to the right, while the mirror hangs on his left. I could go on, but, in short, there is no way that Manny could have seen the mirror image he is supposed to be contemplating.[24] Here, no doubt, we come upon another uncanny visitation from the twilight zone, in which things-changing-places intimate the fantastic intervention of Hitchcock's invisible hand. The manipulativeness of this hand brings out the naturalistically inexpressible psychic rift that Hitchcock wants Manny—and the spectator—to confront. Yet it also announces the faultiness in Hitchcock's own cinema, its incompatibility with transparency, wholeness, and self-identity: virtues of which, not coincidentally, this image aggressively deprives Manny. The doubleness suggests a sense in which Hitchcock may be as much victim as executioner of his unnerving—but far from unerring—touches. The true force of the mirror shot would lie in the fact that continuity itself—be it the self-winding regularity of a wrong man or the no less firmly maintained control of his cinematic master—is a forced untruth.

I privilege these mirrors as examples of continuity errors because in them it is fully apparent that, at bottom, the Hitchcockian Error is *unrectifiable*. The coffee cup might have retained a naturalistic orientation without serious aesthetic damage; frame-painting over the wrong van number would have actually improved the film; and even as they stand, the tiny shift of the one and the gross blunder that is the other both allow us to imagine a film that, at least in principle, *might have* observed the spatiotemporal continuities we imagine operating in real life and therefore in this most "realistic," "topical," and "documentary" of Hitchcock's projects. But to fix the hall-mirror error would obliterate the error's whole reason for being, which is to broach the fantastically uncertain atmosphere that produces nightmares and monsters. And putting the cracked-mirror shot to rights would be even worse: for here, if anywhere, Hitchcock *faces* the Continuity Error—gives it a face and confronts the fact of it—as the truth of his cinema. Assailed by its sudden, startling, painful, unhinging ruptures, the Too-Close Viewer may also face it as what makes Hitchcock's great cinema so distressing to watch: too much like life, this viewer might say, when life refuses to be "lifelike."

Unseen Cameos

Often when I watch a Hitchcock film in this too-close manner, my mind misgives me. I am exhausted by the strain of so much scrutinizing and frustrated by the lapses of attention in which, try as I might to avoid them, I am always catching myself: my task is impossible! I get even sicker of my isolating condition and of the strange, demented feeling that accompanies it: worse than impossible, my task has turned me into a freak! At such tired and lonely moments, I downsize my quest for hidden Hitchcock to the easy, communal version of itself: I search for the cameo.

For here hidden Hitchcock, instead of being the spotty, half-hallucinated phenomenon I experience in solitude, enjoys the reality of a convention acknowledged by audiences all over the world. Looking for the cameo, I become like everyone else in knowing that a Hitchcock film hides an anonymous appearance by its director, typically near the beginning. And better still, everyone else becomes like me in acknowledging the essential secrecy of this cinema, with its artful exploitation of the dominant/recessive polarity in the image. With most viewers, of course, the cameo works to *seal off* Hitchcock's esotericism; since Hitchcock is hiding here, they assume, he will be hidden nowhere else, and if the man is plain to see, the work that goes by his name can hardly prove less so. To me, though, the cameo is heartening in a different way. Here, my laborious, self-doubting search for hidden Hitchcock stands triumphant and sure, a mission accomplished. The cameo thus validates for me the possibility of other, similarly recessed microstructures—and with an equally perverse relation to narrative structure—that I might also successfully identify.

But it is a key part of *The Wrong Man*'s singularity that, for the first and only time since the convention was systematized, Hitchcock *messes with the cameo*. To start with the most obvious modification, the usual frontloading is here taken to the limit. The director appears in the film's very first image, a pre-credit shot in which he declares: "This is Alfred Hitchcock speaking. In the past, I have given you many kinds of suspense pictures; but this time I would like you to see a different one. The difference lies in the fact that this is a true story, every word of it . . ." With this prologue—his sole talking cameo—Hitchcock ends the usual game of hide-and-seek before it can begin, proclaiming his own identity and vouching for the equally straightforward presentation of the story to follow. To Slavoj Žižek, who makes the prologue central to his account of *The Wrong Man*, "I am Alfred Hitchcock" and "This is a true story" promise essentially the same thing: an eschewal of irony, wit, and play as the main determinants of the film's aesthetic structure, which has been relegated, such as it is, to governance by the naked truth. And this relinquishment of style would be, for Žižek, precisely "what's wrong with *The Wrong Man*": conveyed "in a 'direct,' 'serious' way," in an inartistic "metalanguage," the film's message "los[es] its persuasiveness . . . and even the most tragic moments depicted in the film somehow leave us cold."[25]

But Žižek has the wrong idea; in taking the prologue for truth-in-advertising, it is rather he who is being direct, serious, and unpersuasive. Far from being a renunciation of Hitchcockian guile, the opening cameo is this exceptionally devious film's first instance of it. Even if one follows Žižek in taking Hitchcock's speech literally, with no attention to the accompanying music and image, its words remain clotted with equivocation. "This is a true story, every word of it": an extravagant claim that, court transcripts aside, there is no way even to begin verifying. "I have given you many kinds of suspense pictures. This time, I ask you to see a different one." A different kind of suspense picture? Or a picture different *in kind*? Is *The Wrong Man*, finally, a Hitchcock film like all the others—as new, surprising, and different as each of them in its day was said to be—or so absolutely singular in its refusal

3.20 Hitchcock in shadow.

of suspense—"a different *one*" indeed—that it shouldn't be called "a Hitchcock film" at all? One can't help further observing that what Žižek calls Hitchcock's metalanguage is scored to a loud, dissonant motif by Bernard Hermann that has nothing documentary about it. This noirish peal of alarm gives the prologue the familiar acoustics of a narrative emergency, as if some invisible but awful catastrophe had occurred concomitantly with Hitchcock's appearance, or as if this very appearance somehow *were* that catastrophe. The same motif recurs once again—and only once again—during the scene of Manny's incarceration, so that, musically speaking, the film even has Hitchcock *re*appearing in Manny's cell.[26]

But it is the prologue's visual image—the first in the film—that skews the true-story rhetoric most plainly (figure 3.20). The figure whom the Master's unmistakable voice calls "Alfred Hitchcock" is viewed on a sound stage from so far away, and from such a high angle, that all we really see is a squat little man stranded in empty, unbounded space. This man faces us in silhouette, which—itself a shadow—casts before

134

3.21 Title graphic from *The Lodger*.

it a second, inverted shadow that is over twice its size.[27] The commonsense distinction between the stunted, slenderized Man (in all his Pascalian frailty) and his elongated, bulked up Shadow (in full artistic majesty) is visually overridden in the umbrageousness common to both. The inky Gestalt in which both shadows are conjoined—and neither looks right—makes a sort of "long wrong man" out of Hitchcock's very person.

It is not simply that, with its German Expressionist lighting, the shot is full of what we historically understand as "style" in cinema. It is not even that it is full of what we know as style in Hitchcock, whose very first wrong man story, *The Lodger* (1926), featured just such a silhouetting cone of light in its title graphic (figure 3.21), and whose second, *Downhill* (1927), showed the hero preceded on the stairs to his apartment by his own gigantic shadow. What is most striking about this appearance is the fact that, in it, *Hitchcock is unrecognizable.* In contradistinction to the cameos in other films, where it might happen that someone (inattentive or ignorant of the convention) *doesn't* see Hitchcock, here is a cameo in which, though it seems self-evident that Hitchcock stands addressing us, no one *can* see him and hence know for sure. While the composition is classically Hitchcockian, the figure in it, as William Rothman candidly puts it, "could be anyone."[28] In a film about mistaken identity, where people swear that a man is someone he isn't merely on the basis of a similarity of dress and build, it cannot be a negligible fact that, if the well-known voice did not intone, "This is Alfred Hitchcock speaking," we would not be able to identify him any more than we could establish, say, the truth of the film's every word.[29] To what, one may wonder, is this identified, but unidentifiable, double image being "true"?[30]

Recall the pair of cameos in *Strangers on a Train*: the obvious appearance on the train platform that we are all flattered to recognize and the stealthy appearance on Guy's book cover that, if and when we are brought to acknowledge it, rankles with the evidence of something we missed, as Hitchcock meant us to. In *The Wrong Man*, within the confines of a single appearance—an appearance in which all we can say is that Hitchcock *appears to appear*—we deal with a comparably frustrating split. If by his words Hitchcock seems to make himself knowable, as an image—even as a split image—he remains entirely in recalcitrant shadow, literally unforthcoming. On one hand, the man of truth ("I am Alfred Hitchcock, and this is what I will be doing"); on another, the shadow of his style—that is to say, the shadow of a *doubt*, of an enigmatic uncertainty that, dream-wise, floats the identity of people and objects all over the place. In *Strangers'*

3.22 The cameo that wasn't filmed. Licensed by Warner Bros.
Entertainment Inc. All rights reserved.

hidden cameo, we saw Hitchcock, but did not notice him; in
The Wrong Man's obvious cameo, we notice Hitchcock, but
do not see him.

What's more, the prologue is not the only unseen cameo in
the film. Dan Auiler tells us that it replaced another, more
traditional cameo that "Hitchcock decided to cut." Auiler
also claims to have found in the Warner Bros. Archive "an
unused shot" from this cameo, filmed at Bickford's, the cafeteria where Manny has breakfast after work; in this image,
Manny is seated with his newspaper at a small table, while
Hitchcock, also reading a newspaper, stands looming behind
him (figure 3.22).[31] Having found this photograph, too, however, I strongly doubt that it is a photogram—an image that
has been *cut from the film*. The internal evidence is all against

it. Try to visualize the continuity on either side of this essentially static image, its "before" and "after," and you will comprehend the difficulty. Both figures are gripped by an immobilizing absorption (Hitchcock in his newspaper, Manny in his thoughts); neither can have just arrived, or be about to go anywhere. And without such motion, there is simply no way for the cameo to be broken off. The camera, of course, might move instead, but a flashy pan would be out of keeping with the convention's essential discretion, which typically demands that Hitchcock walk briskly into and out of frame; and a cut, too, would underscore rather than underplay the moment. No, this image is only an on-set photograph, intended for publicity purposes, like many other production stills that were routinely taken during the making of Hitchcock's films and in which the director's presence is anything but sly.[32] Unless Auiler is holding out on us, there is no evidence that this Bickford's cameo was ever filmed, or meant to be.

Let me enlarge the importance of this point by turning to another photograph in the Warner Bros. Archive, almost identical to Auiler's in place, angle, and pose, but with certain melodramatic enhancements (figure 3.23). In this version, Manny has a cigarette dangling from his lips, and holds the newspaper's racing section in a closed, unrelaxed grip; his eyes, enlarged, look half hypnotized, half haunted. That this photograph should be a photogram is not simply unlikely; it is impossible. Inserted *anywhere* in the scene at Bickford's, the image would be totally wrong. Its iconography is far closer to the hardened thief who appears at the beginning of *Blackmail* (1929) than to the Manny we see in *The Wrong Man* (figure 3.24). First, Manny doesn't smoke at all in the film, let alone like a gangster or bum. Second, in the many shots of Manny reading his newspaper (in the subway, at

3.23 Auiler photo with enhancements. Licensed by Warner Bros. Entertainment Inc. All rights reserved.

Bickford's, at home) never once does he come close to clutching it so tensely; indeed, whatever the object, his musician's fingers are unfailingly delicate in their handling of it. Third, in the film's chronology, the diner scene falls *before* Manny is falsely accused; in these wee hours at Bickford's, with his coffee, toast, and paper, he still enjoys his undefiled banality. (When the man at the counter asks, "The usual?" there is no little pleasure in Manny's reply: "Same.") Yet the photograph

3.24 The thief in *Blackmail*.

shows us not this comfortable creature of habit, but a veritable man of sorrows. And the nature of his affliction is no less incoherent. Manny looks at once sinister and innocent, both the way the law will depict him—a compulsive gambler "in trouble with the bookies"—and the way we spectators come to know him—the eponymous wrong man charged with crimes he didn't commit. But Manny never was that criminal and isn't yet that wrong man. At this moment in the film, there is no narrative reason for Manny's hypertension.

What *has* induced Manny's altogether wrong expressions of guilt and distress is, apparently, the presence of Hitchcock standing unseen, but not unfelt, behind him—behind his left shoulder, to be exact, which is famously the Devil's place not just in folklore but also in Hitchcockian mythology.[33] Manny and Hitchcock are divided by a central column, which, like the hinge of a diptych, imposes an almost allegorical opposition between the two. One man, gaunt and anguished, seems all expressive "soul," the other, fat and phlegmatic, wholly inert "matter." But the column disappears midway down the photograph, first into the melded shadows of the two men, then behind their bodies; and this invites us to construe a less antithetical, more consubstantial relation between the pair. Though their bodies occupy different perspectival planes (with Manny's face larger than Hitchcock's), they are contiguous on the pictorial surface, where Hitchcock seems to be nudging Manny with his elbow, applying to him a "touch" that galvanizes him as a Hitchcock protagonist with the requisite guilt-ridden agony. Stark opposites have become psychically conjoined twins, as if there were only a limited quantity of matter and anguish to be apportioned between them. Next to the plumped-up Hitchcock, the long lean Manny looks stretched out; and with Manny a nervous wreck, Hitchcock appears to have composure for two. Manny is anxious not only because of Hitchcock, but also, it is suggested, *on his behalf.* No doubt, every Hitchcock appearance performs some such ritual of delegation, whereby the director, refusing all participation in the horrendous adventure he has originated, passes it along to the hapless protagonist who must suffer it in full. If the prologue appearance is excessively tactful in keeping the contaminative Hitchcock from even setting foot in the story world, the Bickford's appearance goes to the opposite extreme in making his active presence in that world so conspicuous that we can hardly believe his real-life protagonist has any existence outside of authorial projection and transference.

And yet the Bickford's cameo, which does not—and could not—appear in the actual film, was seen nonetheless by the first audiences of *The Wrong Man.* Cropped and colorized

3.25 Lobby card.

as the format required, the photograph became one of the
eight so-called lobby cards displayed in the foyers of theaters
where *The Wrong Man* was showing (figure 3.25). Generally,
such cards purported to give viewers an advance look at a
film's key scenes; and though they never bore an exact resemblance to the film's actual images, the discrepancies hardly
posed a problem. The cards were intended to be looked at before the film was projected (when no one had seen the source
images), and perhaps again afterward (when few could remember those images in much detail); they therefore only
needed to be *close enough*, which they generally were. But
with *The Wrong Man*, Hitchcock perverts this preview function. The card in question—number six—promises viewers
a cameo image that they are eventually bound to realize is
missing from the actual film. In this lobby card's eerie light,
the scene at Bickford's seems haunted by a phantom Hitchcock appearance that we are tantalized with envisioning but
never seeing.

Not one, then, but two unseen cameos. Defeated by this twofold invisibility, my eyes feel almost painfully empty; but, vacuumlike, they are also all the readier to be entered and filled by the hidden Hitchcock that—still, they sense!—is in them to find. For if they haven't beheld Hitchcock, they *have* discerned a highly suggestive pattern in his defective appearances. As everyone knows, the Hitchcock cameo typically meets two structural requirements: (1) that Hitchcock *appear* in his film, and (2) that we *recognize* him when he does. *The Wrong Man*'s pair of unseen cameos deform this structure in elegantly opposite ways: the prologue vocally affirms a Hitchcock appearance that cannot be verified visually, while the lobby card gives us a clearly identifiable Hitchcock image that fails to appear in the film. In one case, appearance without recognition; in the other, recognition without appearance. One need not be far advanced in semiotics to theorize a fourth kind of cameo, which would consist in the dialectical negation of *both* typical requirements: a cameo that, while having the formal structure of a recognizable appearance, would also be designed *never to be seen*. In this negative cameo, Hitchcock would be present without seeming to "appear," and, while recognizable, be unlikely ever to *be* recognized. Imagine it: a cameo born—and indeed conceived—to waste its sweetness in the desert air: a cameo that, despite all the art and wit and pain that had gone into its elaboration, and in utter disregard of its very raison d'être, would be simply *thrown away*! It would be as if Hitchcock were saying to himself, plangently, "They *could* recognize me, but they *will* not; here, and forever after, is the proof of their incomprehension."

Now this negative cameo actually exists; it exists, as I have already shown, on the cover of Guy's book in *Strangers on a Train.* But it also exists, in much fiercer and more deeply filmic form, in *The Wrong Man*, where it has lain successfully hidden from viewers since the film's release in 1956; I am about to make it public for the first time. Before I do, let me remark how extraordinary it is that this cameo should have escaped notice for almost sixty years. Amazing that Hitchcock carried this secret to his grave; still more amazing that no actor, no cameraman or crew member, should have breathed a word of it, though some of them had to have been in the know; and most amazing of all that it should have defied the vigilance of Hitchcock critics who, an obsessive lot to begin with, have had home editions of *The Wrong Man* at their disposal for upwards of twenty-five years. All this is only to say that the cameo has been made *singularly* difficult to see; it was only after many, many viewings of "The Long *Wrong Man*" that, by a kind of miracle, I was granted a vision of it. (Another rationale for my "Long *Wrong Man*": miracles happen, as Rose's nurse says in the film, "but it takes time.")

It is not anywhere you might think to look. In vain would you scour the Stork Club, the subway, Bickford's, or any other location appearing "in the first five minutes," as Hitchcock says is his custom in planting the cameo; this cameo has been put off until as late as fifteen minutes from the end of the film. Nor, as is also customary, has it been inserted at a time when no essential plot function requires our attention, such as when Manny first enters the Victor Moore Arcade (and by rights should have crossed paths with Hitchcock rather than the Lookalike). The cameo falls smack in the middle of Manny's trial, at its most dramatic moment.

Scratch that: its *only* dramatic moment. This trial is so miserably short on excitement that, as even Manny has leisure to observe, those in attendance openly yawn, chat, joke, doodle, or freshen lipstick during the proceedings; and the juror who protests the long drawn-out nitpicking ("Your Honor, do we have to sit and listen to all this?") only necessitates a mistrial, to be followed by a retrial that bodes more of the same. For once in the film, it is accurate to say that "every word is true." These lackluster speeches and examinations are lifted verbatim from actual transcripts, which hardly suit a Hollywood courtroom; as Sir John aptly opines in *Murder!*, "the law has no sense of drama." And what trimming there is maladroitly eviscerates the logical structure of legal argument, making the proceedings still more desultory. Worst of all, Hitchcock's camera mimics this listlessness with a lethargy all its own. Again and again, bringing its already plodding movement to virtual stasis, it returns to the same increasingly monotonous set up: a medium close-up of Manny seated in the dock, a scattering of observers behind him. Repeated some twenty-five times throughout the trial with little variation, this "Manny Shot" typically serves as little more than a transition between scenes or a perfunctory focalization within one. And though Manny's expression in it may be called neutral, the shot is the weakest imaginable instance of Hitchcock's beloved "Kuleshov effect," in which an identically repeated face shot takes on different import depending on what the intermediary shots show the eyes seeing.[34] With a single exception, the deployment of the Manny Shot never suggests much responsiveness on Manny's part to what is happening around him: he looks absorbed without being mindful, attentive but not aware. Whether dazed by his unthinkable ordeal, or baffled by the legal niceties being parsed around him, or lost in the mysteries of his rosary, his blank face blocks the process of our projection onto it. Instead, by reverse projection, it draws us into its own inertia; without exactly being an interesting image, it becomes a fascinating one. Looking at the Manny Shot over and over, we enter a fugue state not unlike Manny's *in* the shot: we almost cease to see it.

The exception—which is also the dramatic moment—happens during the D.A.'s examination of one of the insurance company clerks, a Mrs. Ann James. I note that the Manny Shot is unusually dynamic in this scene; far from a free-floating focalization, it functions in a tight shot/countershot alternation whose other term is Mrs. James. For two rounds of this back-and-forth, Manny's eyes are fixed on Mrs. James, whose own eyes, by contrast, skittishly turn everywhere *but* in Manny's direction. The shot of Mrs. James, in other words, is Manny's point of view, but the reverse shot of him is not hers. Then, in the third round:

> **D.A.:** Mrs. James, will you look around this courtroom and tell us if you see the man who was in your office on July 9th in this courtroom?
>
> **MRS. JAMES:** Yes—I do.

For the first time, Mrs. James looks at Manny in the dock; and also for the first time, the reverse Manny Shot, electrified by her words, gets a real emotive charge. While neither Mrs. James nor any other character saw the Manny Shot, it seemed to frame the protagonist as *we* saw him, truly, in all his boring benumbed innocence; but when the Manny Shot becomes her point of view, the identical image frames him in the *other* sense of the word; what had been the right way of seeing him, *while remaining the same image*, makes him look all wrong, uncomfortable in his skin and shifty of eye. It is as if Manny were haplessly absorbing the guilt he sees his accuser see in him. And what constant recurrence had lulled us into thinking of as a stock filler-shot becomes the horrific *Ecce homo* of

Foucaldian discipline: behold your delinquent, just as you've fashioned him! Here is a Kuleshov effect worthy of the name, an image that changes radically in meaning according to its visual context; now, the Manny Shot gains the culminal force of a money shot. If, to recall Žižek's expression, the trial has so far "left us cold," the shock of misrecognition we feel at this climax is genuinely chilling. Hitchcock's classic style consists precisely in such sudden transformations of the banal into the baleful, and the present example is only more sensational for having been long in coming. With this iteration, the Manny Shot thus becomes the director's *Ecce homo*, too, a shot that, by its way of framing Manny as a criminal, draws attention to Hitchcock as an artist.[35]

And in more ways than one. *Do you see this man?* There came a time I will now tell of when, at last hearing the doubleness in the question, I *did* see; and unlike Mrs. James, I didn't just see Manny; I also saw, peeping behind Manny's right shoulder like a wary rabbit from its hole, the face of Alfred Hitchcock (figure 3.26; 1:29:29–30). At the sight—so long expected, but still utterly startling—how my heart pounded, my skin tingled with the thrill! And despite the watery film that, whether from the strength of my emotion, or from the necessity to wash away a foreign body, now began to coat my eyes, they felt so tightly "glued to the screen" that there no longer seemed the slightest distance between it and them, or between Hitchcock and me. I had at last achieved (if anyone ever did) that complete coalescence with the author that was the goal and limit of my too-close viewing: Hitchcock had a Secret, and it was mine! And yet, somehow, as if it were Hitchcock who had just caught *me* looking rather than vice versa, I felt less in joyful possession of this Secret than helplessly, even painfully, possessed by it. Again, it fit me like a glove,

3.26 The courtroom cameo.

but what glove is never too tight? I had got unduly close, not for knowledge, but for any breathable comfort in the knowledge; I knew too much, too much for my own good. I would have recoiled, but I could no more turn my eyes from this rending vision than Melanie Daniels could turn hers from the mass of crows overspreading a schoolyard jungle gym. Powerless even to pause or rewind, I could only stare and keep the avenue of this dreadful, repugnant intimacy wide open.

But in under half a second I was staring at nothing; the camera had already cut back to the witness stand. The D.A. now asked Mrs. James to step down and point "the man" out to us. "*Right there!*" she replied without budging. His question became more insistent: "Would you step down and put your hand on his shoulder?" As she swiveled her head in vain appeal to the judge, the Manny Shot returned for my further inspection: Hitchcock was no longer anywhere to be found (1:29:38–39)! Had I been seeing things in my inordinate desire to see *the* thing? And was I now awakened to honest if dull reality? But no: when, turning her eyes back on Manny,

Mrs. James did step down, the Manny Shot returned once more, and there again was Hitchcock at his lapine peeping, as if to say, in the very low voice that only the closest confidant ever hears: "You were right; it's just as you dreamed" (1:29:48–49).

And just as in a dream, the camera took him away once more, in favor of Mrs. James as she proceeded through the courtroom and laid her hand on Manny's shoulder, the same shoulder that had been hiding Hitchcock behind its back (1:29:59). For the first time, I noticed that this shot showed nothing of Manny except a remarkably generic shoulder; and that, in the following reaction shot, Manny's eyes—which I had always assumed were looking *at* his shoulder—were instead glancing aversively away from it. One moment the shoulder was the only part of Manny we *could* see and the next it had become the thing that no one, including Manny himself, *should* see. To whom else might this "loose," oneirically dislocated shoulder be attached? What other touch could it be thus cross-referencing? For under the cameo's pressure, this Laying-on of the Hand had jumped out of the narrative into another, far stranger scene in which the performer as well as the recipient of the touch had acquired uncanny new identities. Mrs. James was no longer just touching Manny, she was also touching Hitchcock, who was right behind Manny; and she was touching me, who had just been found guilty of looking at what I wasn't supposed to see there. And Hitchcock was touching me, and I was touching him, vividly *holding* one another (the metaphor seemed to have risen from the grave) in a frightened, frozen, and yet deeply desiring, mutual gaze.

Then the scene was over, and with it, all the dramatic interest of the trial. But the Manny Shot, back to its old job as a factotum punctuation mark, kept on coming, and every time it did, I had eyes only for the little bit of screen above Manny's right shoulder. In the first recurrence, that space was occupied by the head of a balding old man craning forward to see more clearly; I wouldn't, unassisted by my remote, swear that it was or wasn't Hitchcock. In the second recurrence, this man was even harder to see; and in the third, he was no longer visible at all. Finally, however, Manny looked over his own shoulder, and I got a good close look at the man. No way! He bore so little resemblance to Hitchcock that for a moment I again wondered if, in believing I saw Hitchcock in the first place, I hadn't been the victim of short-sightedness together with a vivid imagination; could it have been this nondescript geezer all along? And, as if cued to my doubt, the man, the Manny Shot, the courtroom itself—all vanished from sight; the juror had misspoken, the trial was canceled, the film moved on. The rabbit, having rematerialized, turned into a dove; the dove flew away; and so ended the conjuring trick.

Since the viewing I have just narrated, I have made it my repeated employment to rewind, slow, step, and pause this hidden courtroom cameo. I sum up so my readers may, by performing these same actions, verify what is Hitchcock's most furtively structured appearance. At its kernel is the appearance proper in which, seated behind Manny, Hitchcock appears, vanishes, and reappears. The pattern is cunningly extended by means of a Hitchcock stand-in who, ensconced where the real one had been sitting, likewise appears, disappears, and reappears. And to notice so much will lead one also to notice, *before* the appearance proper, a man sitting in Hitchcock's future place; he too is sometimes just visible, sometimes not at all, but never so much as to allow us to know whether he is Hitchcock, the geezer, or someone else entirely. In short, the courtroom cameo takes the form of a triple oscillation, between Hitchcock's presence and absence; between his facsimiles' presence and absence; and, of course, between Hitchcock and his facsimiles.

We have already observed this cameo's anomaly of placement; but its own structure is no less odd. The regular cameo in Hitchcock is continuous, confined to a single shot, or at most two contiguous shots that combine in a clear unity, as in *Shadow of a Doubt*. But here, Hitchcock (or his stand-in) is shuttled in and out of the visual field, and the shuttling is itself staggered over several shots. This is not a moment of surprise, but a rhythm of startlement. Different from the phenomenon of merely multiple cameos (found in *The Lodger*, *Rope*, *Strangers on a Train*, and, of course, *The Wrong Man*), the courtroom cameo evinces an *inner* multiplicity. I am reminded of what linguistics calls "the frequentative," a verbal inflection (e.g., Latin *-itare*, English *-le* or *-er*) that expresses an action's intrinsic intermittence. Accordingly, this appearance would be not so much an act as an agitation; not a momentary crack in the narrative surface but a spasmodic crackling.

One frequentative does particular justice to the cameo's affinity with cinema-as-violence: the appearance *flickers*, as if the punctual "flick of the knife" that Rupert envisions in *Rope* had become the slashing that both effects and edits Marion's murder in *Psycho*.[36] You'll recall that the neon cameo in *Rope* also flickered, revealing the same Hitchcock image every time it flashed. And so it is with the courtroom cameo, as a bit more too-close viewing lets us see: Hitchcock's two sneak looks are actually a single rear projection repeated behind slightly dissimilar foregrounds. (No wonder no one on the set seems to have witnessed the cameo; it only happened on the editing table!) But the point of the trick is to get us to construe even an exact replication as a different image. The ostensible variance then feeds into the subsequent confusion that develops between the real McCoy and his decoy. In this way, the cameo gives impetus to seeing—and playing—the maddening wrong-man game that the film sets up not just around Manny, but also around Hitchcock, of whom there are almost as many possible stand-ins in the film as there are, say, tall men of Manny's age wearing hats and overcoats.

Like the transference in the Arcade, the courtroom cameo perpetuates a fundamental Hitchcock convention in se-cret, hidden by the realism of the film's world and running speed. Without such camouflage, would *The Wrong Man* be just a normal Hitchcock film, cameo and all? But, like the Arcade transference in this, too, the courtroom cameo only preserves its respective convention by fuzzing its contours so that it seems, even when visible, unstable. The cameo, in other words, maps out a further patch of that defective dot-to-dot puzzle in which the film encourages us to draw doubtful connections between images, connections that, no matter how wrong they may prove on being scrutinized, cannot be clearly separated from the right connections we also are invited to make; nor can they be ever cleanly ex-punged from our experience of a design whose rightness, or indeed, whose very legibility, is thus being increasingly over-whelmed by so many irreconcilable lines. Without its real-ist camouflage, then, *The Wrong Man* would *not* be a normal Hitchcock; it would be the normal Hitchcock afflicted with diplopia—that double vision in which what we suppose is one object appears confusingly as more than one. It is the normal Hitchcock in the course of losing its mind, and even its shape, which keeps falling into self-inconsistency right before our eyes. This derangement is what you see—not to mention what you risk contracting—if you look long and close enough.[37]

Credits

In work by others, I have often been struck by the sneaky (dialectical?) tendency of acknowledgments to run counter to a book's mood and even principles. And so it is here: the Too-Close Viewer, self-proclaimed social isolate, admits to having been thickly surrounded by aiders and abettors.

It was the students in my Hitchcock courses to whom I first previewed much of this book; they formed a decidedly interactive audience, whose visual intelligence confirmed, corrected, and otherwise advanced my thinking. Let me particularly acknowledge the sharp-eyed Edy Beteran, Megan Grint, Jordan Klein, Jed Pennington, Rohan Ramakrishnan, and Rose Roark. In Jonathan Larner-Lewis, John Lurz, and Brandon White, I had the benefit of uncommonly congenial assistants, always expeditious at getting me materials I wanted and often mediumistic at putting me in contact with those I hadn't known to ask for.

I always seem to be thanking these same people: Lee Edelman, Amanpal Garcha, David Kurnick, Franco Moretti, Laura Mullen, and Alex Woloch; their work and conversation remain provocative agents in my writing. Other support—intellectual, moral, and sometimes truly "whatever"—has come from Matt Bell, Lawrence Benn, Fareed Ben-Youssef, Stephen Best, Robert Buck, Eric Burstyn, Carol Christ, Suzanne Daly, Frances Ferguson, Philip Fisher, Thomas Hostetter, Marianne Kaletzky, Andrew Klevan, Joseph Litvak, Alison MacKeen, Karla Oeler, Samuel Otter, Richard Peña, Kent Puckett, Elaine Scarry, Elizabeth Simpson, Jerrine Tan, Kevin Thomas, Traye Turner, Yoshifumi Uehara, Rebecca Walkowitz, Rob White, Kim Whitworth, Wendy Xin, and Damon Young. At the Warner Bros. Archive in Los Angeles, Jonathan Auxlier benevolently guided me through the dark forest of materials on *The Wrong Man*. And at the University of Chicago Press, Susan Bielstein took charge and care of this book as only a fellow Hitchcockophile could. For their expert assistance with design and editorial, I thank her colleagues Michael Brehm, Joel Score, and James Whitman Toftness; and for his tireless help with the cover image, Universal archivist Peer Ebbighausen.

Paramount to the realization of this study were three pairs of "second eyes." One belongs to Martin Zirulnik, who gave my Hitchcock viewing the advantage of his own peerless monocle. Another belongs to Ramsey McGlazer, who, at every stage of composition, focused on my manuscript the laser beam of his superbly close editorial and critical attention. And the third belongs to Garrett Stewart, who was unfailingly ready to refract any part of my text through the brilliant prism of his commentary; over and over, his iridescent vision encouraged me to attempt something more worthy of it. To this dear reader, *Hidden Hitchcock* is gratefully dedicated.

Notes

PREVIEW

1. William Rothman, *The Murderous Gaze*, 2nd ed. (Albany: State University of New York Press, 2012), 109.

2. Raymond Bellour's superfine analysis of the Prairie Stop sequence in *North by Northwest* (1959) is, in every sense, the best example. In demonstrating the astonishingly exhaustive structural network whose intricate repetitions and symmetries catch every detail, no matter how minute, in a classically Oedipal narrative of couple-formation, it replicates the twin mainstays of Hitchcock's manifest style—the marriage plot and the preeminent legibility— in dazzling critical-theoretical guise. Concomitantly, thanks to this alignment, what might seem fanatical in Bellour's excessively precise critical performance disappears in the light of its manifest hermeneutic serviceability, not unlike the way that L. B. Jefferies's compulsive voyeurism is validated when it leads him to solve a murder in *Rear Window* (1954). Just as Hitchcock makes amends for his own withdrawal from the social field by providing us with sociable plots and universally legible structures, so Bellour would redeem his analytic excesses with a complete or decisive interpretation destined to circulate in film criticism as the coin of its realm. The fascinated drive to scrutiny that (more or less avowedly) inspires him is never visible as the gratuitous or arbitrary nature of his analytical results,

which, on the contrary, are rightly admired for their "rigor." See Raymond Bellour, "Symbolic Blockage," trans. Mary Quaintance, in *The Analysis of Film*, ed. Constance Penley (Bloomington: Indiana University Press, 2000), 77–192.

3. See Thomas M. Leitch, *Find the Director and Other Hitchcock Games* (Athens, GA: University of Georgia Press, 1991).

4. I have committed a sort of terminological *continuity error* in these essays. The first essay, on *Strangers on a Train* (1951), gels around the notion of too-close *reading*, while the latter two center on what in them gets called too-close *viewing*. I regret the inconsistency— or rather, regret that it was not amenable to being standardized after the fact. But it appears to be the cost of (what I don't regret) my allegiance to the essay form, which demands an unrepeatable—and even irremediable—immersion in "the matter in hand." In *Strangers*, the dominant metaphor through which Hitchcock reflects upon his esoteric art is that of reading a book. He figures this art as a hidden pair of Hitchcock-edited anthologies, which some people (such as Guy and the ordinary spectator) must fail to read, and others (like Bruno and the Too-Close Reader) may read all too well. I adopted his metaphor the more readily owing to certain contemporary accounts of "reading" that I wanted to engage in implicit debate: Moretti's "distant reading," Best and Marcus's "surface reading," and, in Hitchcock studies particularly, Cohen's "cryptonymies." See Stephen Best and Sharon Marcus, "Surface Reading: An Introduction," *Representations*, no. 108 (2009), 1–21; Franco Moretti, *Distant Reading* (London: Verso, 2013); and Tom Cohen, *Hitchcock's Cryptonymies*, 2 vols. (Minneapolis: University of Minnesota Press, 2005).

In *Rope* (1948), however, the Book's pride of place as a mise-en-abyme is held by Painting. Though the film puts piles of books on display, none is meant to be read, only to be looked at by a collector of first editions. Instead, it is the picturocentric dialogue ("painting the picture and not hanging it," "making our work of art a masterpiece," "the finishing touch") that most saliently carries the film's ruling preoccupations with the perfect crime and a perfectionist cinema. *The Wrong Man* (1956), too, hinging on what it may entail to *look at* a man who *looks like* another man, similarly foregrounds visual over textual self-reflexiveness. Still letting Hitchcock guide me, but in these cases along a rather different path, I came to feel that *viewing an image* was a more serviceable description of what I was doing than *reading a text*—and not just literally, but also because the process gave a greater role to chance or incidental observations; unlike reading, at least to one of my generation, viewing did not seem essentially indentured to the aim of interpreting a work or discovering its logical necessity. At the start of *The Sight of Death*, his intensive record of the process of seeing, again and again, a pair of Poussin landscapes, T. J. Clark points out that he never gives an overall first "reading" of the paintings that he will keep coming back to look at, implying that reading and looking would lead him, at least initially, in different directions. See T. J. Clark, *The Sight of Death* (New Haven, CT: Yale University Press, 2006), 9. The slippage of my terms may well bear out this implication, but what matters more, I hope, is the "too-closeness" common to both ways of proceeding, which should ultimately enable them to take us, Proust-wise, to some, if not all, of the same places. Even in *Strangers*, Hitchcock is at once the author of the Book and the Image on its back cover.

5. Rothman probably doesn't see the ballot because he is concentrating on the camera's presentation of the protagonist, which is always a key site for his reflections on Hitchcock's authorship. In his own account of the jury room scene, for instance, Rothman does give us the close observation that, alone among the twelve jurors, Sir John is absent from the frame until the foreman says, "There's just Sir John," and he at last comes in view.

6. Laura Mulvey, *Death 24x a Second: Stillness and the Moving Image* (London: Reaktion, 2006), 166.

7. Roland Barthes, *Mythologies*, trans. Annette Lavers (New York: Hill and Wang, 1972), 130.

8. Stephen Booth, *Precious Nonsense* (Berkeley: University of California Press, 1998), 6, 16, passim. With kindred imagination, Tom Cohen has found a cornucopia of verbal puns in Hitchcock's work. See Cohen, *Hitchcock's Cryptonymies*. But film studies hasn't yet theorized Booth's sense of nonsense on the strictly visual plane.

9. Of course, all of this would have looked different in 1957, the year Rohmer and Chabrol published the first critical book on Hitchcock. Necessarily stopping before *Vertigo* (1958) and its successors, the French critics conclude their survey with *The Wrong Man*, "a film that not only brings together the themes scattered throughout his

work, but also eloquently proves that the attempt to illuminate the depths of his work was worth the effort." Eric Rohmer and Claude Chabrol, *Hitchcock: The First Forty-Four Films*, trans. Stanley Hochman (New York: Continuum, 1988), 145.

HIDDEN PICTURES

1. Allen's phrase, with its useful emphasis, comes from *Hitchcock's Romantic Irony* (New York: Columbia University Press, 2007), 21.

2. In *Find the Director and Other Hitchcock Games*, Leitch argues that "it is the audience's desire for pleasure . . . that gives the cameos their point" (4). His claim seems to be true as far as it goes, by which I mean—and will be showing—that this Hitchcock game goes further than notions of "pleasure" and "point" take us.

3. Anthony Shaffer in "The Story of *Frenzy*," a documentary included in *Frenzy* (1972; University City, CA 2000) DVD.

4. In print, I mean. But on celluloid, there is room to wonder. The first scene of François Ozon's *Swimming Pool* (2003) alludes to the opening conversation in *Strangers*, and seems to reflect on the two Hitchcock appearances (the hidden celebrity photograph, the unrecognized passerby) that frame it. The detective novelist Sarah Morton is being accosted by a fellow tube-rider who is reading one of her stories and has identified her from the author photo:

> **TUBE-RIDER:** Excuse me, but aren't you Sarah Morton? It *is* you. I recognize you. Look, I'm reading your latest novel. I love it. I'm a big fan of Inspector Dorwell. I've read all your books—
> **SARAH MORTON:** You must have mistaken me for someone else. I'm not the person you think I am. Excuse me *(leaves the train)*.

In an obvious sense, the reprise is a reversal. Morton *is* recognized as an author, though she doesn't want to be; and if, as one can't help thinking, Hitchcock *would* like to be recognized as an author, and not just a fat man, he has made this almost impossible. But both authors are bent on affirming, against the common perception of them, an unknown self and a secret writing.

5. Which, of course, puts us in a version of Guy's plight. The famous tennis player is so used to being recognized that when Bruno says, "Aren't you Guy Haines?" he need answer only with a fatuously

benevolent smile. But all smiles stop together when he loses his alibi because—in an amazing reversal of his habitual good fortune—the drunken Professor Collins *doesn't know who he is*, and so doesn't remember meeting him on the train, and so can't back up his story. Like Hitchcock in the appearance, or like Bruno who must wear his name on a tie clip, Guy is made to inhabit the abject condition of nonrecognition.

6. Andrew Sarris, "Hitchcock," in *Focus on Hitchcock*, ed. Albert J. LaValley (Englewood Cliffs, NJ: Prentice-Hall, 1972), 88.

7. Bill Krohn, *Hitchcock at Work* (London: Phaidon, 2000), 124.

8. A while ago, the blogosphere was percolating with conjecture that Hitchcock had made an appearance in drag in *North by Northwest*. Closer attention reveals that the lady in question is not Hitchcock, but Jesslyn Fax, the actress who plays the sculptress in *Rear Window*. And yet the pointed gratuitousness of the camera's focus on her unites with her own direct look at *us* to make the moment formally evocative of a Hitchcock appearance.

I note in this regard that Michelangelo Antonioni, whose cinema so plainly proffers itself as a modernist cover version of Hitchcock's, also teases us with a female Hitchcock cameo. In the near-empty park that will become a putative murder scene, the photographer-protagonist of *Blow-Up* (1966) crosses paths with a portly woman of a certain age wearing a suit, tie and hat. With familiarly pear-shaped insouciance, she picks up bits of litter with a speared stick, a cleverly reversed citation of Hitchcock's appearance littering a London street in *The 39 Steps* (1935). And however factitious, Antonioni's Hitchcock passes the protagonist in the genuine Hitchcock manner: with no acknowledgement from either party. Here, the personal invisibility implicit in *Hitchcock's* "Hitchcock cameo" gestures toward a collective alienation.

9. One of many examples: as the train is pulling into Metcalf, a bulky man may be observed just starting to emerge from the shadows on screen right; it might be Hitchcock, who in the very next shot comes on the platform from that direction, as if continuing the movement. But it isn't; the first man does not carry a bass, and Hitchcock is wearing a suit of a different shade.

10. Even with the surrogate, however, a similar problem may be seen to arise. Like the cameo, the surrogate is never unambig-

uously singular, and it too enjoys an essentially *doubtful* distribution. In *Strangers*, for instance, one critic will maintain that Hitchcock is Bruno, while another, equally persuasive, will contend that Hitchcock is the anonymous passerby who causes Bruno to drop his lighter. Once you start considering the many such claims, along with the prospects that may be suggested by your own ingenuity, you will find your list of surrogates expanding to become virtually coterminous with the entire character-field. Whereupon the notion of a surrogate will have lost its utility and meaning together: to find "Hitchcock" everywhere is no better than not finding him at all.

11. François Truffaut, "A Certain Tendency of the French Cinema," in *Movies and Methods: An Anthology*, vol. 1, ed. Bill Nichols (Berkeley: University of California Press, 1976), 224–37.

12. Eric Rohmer, "Roberto Rossellini: *Stromboli*," in *The Taste for Beauty*, trans. Carol Volk (Cambridge: Cambridge University Press, 1989), 126.

13. The claim straddles two oppositions:

Author/compiler. Strictly speaking, Hitchcock is not the author of this anthology, but only its compiler. Given that the front cover bears the title "Alfred Hitchcock's Book of Suspense" (like "Alfred Hitchcock's *Strangers on a Train*" in the credits); that the back cover features Hitchcock's picture in the author's place; and that the inside contents are framed by his preface, the distinction seems to entail no difference. And yet it also has the merit of glancing at a certain "anthologizing" tendency in the film's own handling of suspense. As is well known, Hitchcock conceived *Strangers* as a return to form after the back-to-back failures of *Under Capricorn* (1949) and *Stage Fright* (1950). Under pressure to offer not a new invention but an inventory of old ones, he structured this comeback as a succession of set pieces, a virtual digest of suspense effects and devices.

Author/plagiarist. To recognize the *Fireside Book* is also to know that Hitchcock got the idea for it from an earlier cinematic encounter between strangers on a train in *Leave Her to Heaven* (John S. Stahl, 1945). The observation-car gods have seated a handsome young man (Cornell Wilde) across the aisle from a beautiful young woman (Gene Tierney). The Tierney character has her head in a book that the Wilde character, who is its author, recognizes by his face on the back cover; introductions follow, with fatal consequences. Hitchcock, in hiding his own author photograph, necessarily conceals this borrowing as well. But if we catch the steal, it only points up the perverse originality of his authorial self-presentation. In *Leave Her to Heaven*, the author photo is hardly more than a clever plot device; and the fact of Wilde's authorship is a purely thematic element, one among many iterations of the male authority destined to be undermined by the psychopathic Tierney. In *Strangers*, the author photo not only does no narrative service; it makes the narrative incoherent; and the citation from *Heaven*, once recognized, makes this loose screw even looser, nonsensically inviting us to see Hitchcock, Banquo-like, hovering in the seat Bruno has taken over from the former film's author figure.

14. In *Spellbound* (1945) he carries a violin case, in *The Paradine Case* (1947) a covered cello, in *Vertigo* a horn case. *Rear Window* puts his appearance in a musician's apartment, and *Topaz* (1969) scores it to the theme song from *Alfred Hitchcock Presents*. It is as if his direction were being imaged as a performing art, the rendering of a preexisting score.

15. As it happens, "The Band Played On" gets replayed during Miriam's murder, underlining the refused word-image correspondence for a second time. Whether singing or being strangled to the tune, this poor girl never shakes with alarm.

16. A pair of examples. First, from *The Man Who Knew Too Much* (1956):

> JO CONWAY (on arriving at the luxurious Mamounia Hotel): Well, this eases the pain!
> HANK: What pain, Mummy?
> JO: It's just an expression, honey.

Second, from *Psycho* (1960):

> SAM LOOMIS: You're alone here, aren't you?
> NORMAN BATES: Mmm-hmm.
> SAM: Drive me crazy.
> NORMAN: I think that would be a rather extreme reaction, don't you?
> SAM: Just an expression.

In both cases, the narrative proceeds to literalize the figure of speech. When Hank is kidnapped from the Mamounia, Jo is given sedatives,

162 / NOTES TO PAGES 46–52

as a prospective amputee might be given whiskey, to relieve the anticipated acuteness of her pain; and a forensic psychiatrist is on hand at the end of *Psycho* to establish Norman as certifiably insane.

17. The literalized tracking has been noticed, if not discussed, by Sabrina Barton; the literalized shots, by Tom Cohen. See Sabrina Barton, "'Crisscross': Paranoia and Projection in *Strangers on a Train*," in *Out in Culture: Gay, Lesbian and Queer Essays on Popular Culture*, ed. Corey K. Creekmur and Alexander Doty (Durham, NC: Duke University Press, 1995), 220; and Cohen, *Hitchcock's Cryptonymies*, 2:30.

18. If too-close reading is too close to belong to the old-time religion of the Reading, it is also too close to find sufficient justification in the new theology of Theory. Game theory, for instance, has allowed Thomas M. Leitch to say many interesting things about the Hitchcock appearance, but his model, in which "the audience's desire for pleasure . . . gives the cameos their point" would never allow us to recognize the hidden pictures, which mar both the pleasure and the point of "finding the director." See Leitch, *Find the Director*, 5. Likewise, Tom Cohen has proven a brilliant adept in what he theorizes as Hitchcock's "cryptonymies," secret words that run through Hitchcock's oeuvre, where they point to the conditions of the visual in a primordial linguistic inscription. Yet while these always-outré cryptonymies shock and awe Cohen's readers, Cohen himself remains completely unfazed by his discoveries, apparently unaware of—and certainly never sharing—the vertigo they invariably occasion in others. This shocking work cannot recognize shock, let alone experience it. That is because, for Cohen, these "secret names" never name any genuine secrets; the *mathesis universalis* of poststructuralism has already penetrated them thoroughly. In consequence, his account of Hitchcock must occlude a charade that is not the simple effect of a rigorously foreordained problematic, and emerges instead from experiential peculiarities. See Cohen, *Hitchcock's Cryptonymies*.

19. The proliferation of Hitchcock "possibles" throughout the film ministers to the same fantasy of touching him; it is as though we were put in a game of tag that could only end when we laid hold of "the real one."

20. Philip Fisher's discussion of "the modern spiritualization of

fear in the sublime" helps us measure how far Hitchcock is from sharing any Romantic or Kantian tendency in this regard. See Philip Fisher, *The Vehement Passions* (Princeton, NJ: Princeton University Press, 2003), 146–50.

21. Indeed, it was in the course of speaking to Ernest Lehman about playing the audience "like a giant organ" that Hitchcock broached his idea of a literally electrifying cinema. See Donald Spoto, *The Dark Side of Genius* (New York: Ballantine, 1983), 440; and also Lee Edelman, *No Future* (Durham, NC: Duke University Press, 2004), 81.

UNDERSTYLE

1. Pascal Bontizer on Hitchcockian suspense: "Everything is proceeding normally, according to routines that are ordinary, even humdrum and unthinking, until someone notices that an element in the whole, because of its inexplicable behavior, is a stain. The entire sequence of events unfolds from that point." Pascal Bonitzer, "Hitchcockian Suspense," trans. Martin Thom, in *Everything You Always Wanted to Know about Lacan (But Were Afraid to Ask Hitchcock)*, ed. Slavoj Žižek (London: Verso, 1992), 20. *Rope*'s plot essentially reverses the priorities of this schema: for Rupert, no doubt, it is the murder that is discovered hidden in the mundane, but for the spectator, it is the mundane—in the form of the party—that is summoned into being so that the murder has something to pervert or "stain." *Rope* thus clarifies the real function of social banality in Hitchcock, which is not to *hide* the crime (which would be much better hidden here without the party), but to *extend* the crime as a spoiling of quotidian reality. By means of the party, which is both Brandon's idea and Hitchcock's, the crime transcends its particularity in a universality of ramification. Compare the end of *The Birds* when, instead of the words "The End," we are given the Universal logo.

2. His point is similar to the one Leonard will make in *North by Northwest*: "I've never trusted neatness; neatness is always the result of deliberate planning."

3. This, one might say, is Hitchcock to the letter! Though the party guests may be innocent of any suspicion of a pun here, no one can claim that *Rope*'s spectators are equally clueless. When Rupert is given David's hat by mistake, the camera zeroes in on the

D.K. monogram inscribed on the inside lining. As Rupert grasps this proof of Brandon's foul play, *we* get confirmation of his equally foul pun. Was it for this that Hitchcock changed the victim's name from Ronald Kentley (in the source play) to David?

4. Likewise the writer of *Rope*, the novelization published on the film's release. See *Rope* (New York: Dell, 1948). This anonymous hack, committed to representing what we see onscreen as faithfully as a purely linguistic description can, includes Brandon's first correction of the candle, but not the second nor any of the business that follows it. Did our ghost writer fail to see these things? Or did he simply decide they were needlessly complicating?

5. *Rope* did in fact have a script girl; it was Charlsie Bryant (*The Sting* [1973], *Jaws* [1975]) on her first assignment, but Hitchcock does not list her in the credits.

6. A good example of this rigged rivalry is *Dial M for Murder*, whose very plot allegorizes it. Tony Wendice beautifully masterminds the murder of his wife and, when she kills her would-be killer instead, makes even more artful rearrangements to pin the crime on her. But this same murder-mystery-ish cleverness allows Mark Halliday, her lover and an actual mystery writer, to figure out Tony's scheme without so much as suspecting him; from there it's a small step to incriminating him. Broadly considered, Tony's defeat is a generic one: he can never stand a chance in a film whose success as a murder mystery depends on its protagonist's failure at murder. But, considered in detail, as a series of discrete slips, his undoing also pays antiphrastic tribute to the unerring touch, the unbroken sostenuto, of Hitchcock's manifest style.

7. David Bordwell, *Poetics of Cinema* (New York: Routledge, 2008), 37.

8. Rohmer and Chabrol, *Hitchcock: The First Forty-Four Films*, 90–91.

9. This is a bizarre claim to make in any case. Most viewers would agree that the overt cuts are at least as conspicuous as the covert ones; in their very rarity, they deliver the radical jolt of montage.

10. V. F. Perkins, "*Rope*," *Movie* 7 (1963): 11–13.

11. Philippe Mather, "Shot Transitions and Narrative Logic in Hitchcock's *Rope*," *Kinema* (Spring 2009), http://www.kinema .uwaterloo.ca/article.php?id=446&feature.

12. Here he might have used a little imagination. After all, the motivation for the cuts arises as a question only through the monotony of their pretext. This so-called problem would never have existed if Hitchcock had varied the objects on which the fade to black occurs—as he easily could have done: Mrs. Wilson, for example, is actually wearing a black dress. In "Anal *Rope*," to unriddle the matter, I proposed linking the camera's obsessive fondness for men's backs (of which even the back of the cassone, given what it contains, is another example) to the repressed homosexual desire awakened in the film by its closeted protagonists. See D. A. Miller, "Anal *Rope*," *Representations*, no. 32 (1990), 114–33. But the suggestion remains as alien to film studies as ever it was. Writing over forty years ago, François Truffaut limited *Rope*'s homosexuality to the observation that the protagonists were "two young homosexuals." François Truffaut with Helen G. Scott, *Hitchcock* (New York: Simon & Schuster, 1984), 179. Writing in 2008, David Bordwell confines it to the identification of the protagonists as "two gay college men." Bordwell, *Poetics of Cinema*, 33. The only thing that has changed is the dubious new qualification of Brandon and Philip as graduates. (The film is silent on their baccalaureates, and in the 1948 novelization, only Philip had completed college.) I prefer the candor shown on this point by Rohmer and Chabrol, who, having remarked the murderers' homosexuality, add this caution: "Let us not allow ourselves to be too fascinated by this latter key. . . . [I]t closes more doors than it opens." See Rohmer and Chabrol, *Hitchcock: The First Forty-Four Films*, 91. For who can help defying this exhortation, whose very authors have already defied it with their too fascinated trope of an aperture that will and shall remain closed to the homosexual key?

Viewed as a sexual preference, male homosexuality is obviously a marginal phenomenon in Hitchcock's largely hetero-themed oeuvre; but it becomes considerably more suggestive when understood (as it is at every level of culture) as an insistence on the eroticized anus. Start counting up the many objects in the film that go from a retentive, integral state to an expulsive, ruptured, or sullied one: the firmly closed chest that ejects the rope; the "good crystal" that cracks in Philip's hand; the clean/encrusted candles, the neat/messy apartment, the piled/scattered books, the binding/slackening rope. Such objects may not be exceptional in Hitchcock's films, but their sheer number in *Rope* surely is, and they receive a unique formalization from the hidden cuts, in which continuity indulges the fissure as its open secret. Not for nothing does Janet say she is employed by "an untidy little magazine known as *Allure*"; it is precisely to the allure of the untidy that Hitchcock succumbs in *Rope*. He violates his usual proctophobic perfectionism so repeatedly here that it seems little more than the ruse of an anal jouissance.

Yet, though in this sense the present essay may be read as an extension of "Anal *Rope*," it seems truer to admit that it represents a calculated failure to follow through on that first essay. Twenty years ago, when the homosexuality of Brandon and Philip was a contentious issue for viewers (many of whom didn't see it and didn't want to), it seemed important to theorize the connotative field in which Hitchcock secretly pursued this theme, and to make his camera's arbitrary-seeming predilection for men's backs comprehensible within that field. But such an approach to *Rope* now has the disadvantage of being obvious, to me if not to Mather or Bordwell. By a familiar dialectical reversal, instead of stimulating me to too-close viewing as it once did, it has come to stand in the way of all that too-close viewing might allow me to see.

13. Despite this bit of malice, Perkins's observations have the merit of being true to what we see. By contrast, Mather seems to be imposing on *Rope* an immutable cinematic code that he may then fault the film for failing to observe. In a work as formally original as *Rope*, it is hardly beyond the realm of possibility that the fade to black—here, not imposed on the narrative from the outside, but finding its occasion within the mise-en-scène itself—is being resignified. Granted, we experience a peculiar disorientation during the cuts: should we try and see them or try and ignore them? But "temporal confusion" plays no part in this disturbance; have even casual viewers thought that narrative time was broken off in the blackouts? On the contrary, the back-blackout is so legible a sign of continuity that, only five years after *Rope*, Robert Aldrich used the device on popular television to signify his story's unbroken temporal flow on either side of a commercial ("The Hard Way," *Four-Star Playhouse*, 1953). He may have been poaching on Hitchcock, or he may have been simply borrowing from theatrical tradition, in which a formal blackout, sometimes in the form of a curtain, between

otherwise continuous acts is hardly unknown. (Even as archaic a form as Bunraku resorts to black as the sign of a pause, rather than a break, in narrative time. While narrator and shamisen player are being changed for a new pair of performers, the puppets are turned away from us, so that all we see is the puppeteers' black robes; when the new chanter and musician are in place, the puppets are turned toward us again, and the drama resumes where it left off.) Let me further note against Mather that since *every* special effect is "showing off," it necessarily evinces an excess of visual flair over narrative justification and is open to a similar charge of being "annoying."

14. Nowadays, of course, what I am calling the monocle is backed up by a whole digital technology that confirms and extends its vision. But the monocle must not be understood as either a mystification of that technology, naïvely projecting it backward as Hitchcock's artistic intention, or an abuse of it, hacking into data inimical to that intention. Even in the epoch before VHS, to watch a Hitchcock film was always to dream of inspecting its images ad libitum—and critics who worked with a print at their disposal typically did just that. A DVD player now lets everyone scrutinize Hitchcock's esoteric images, but the desire to engage the game of hide-and-seek latent in them—a game made just barely visible during theatrical projection—is born with the films themselves.

15. Roland Barthes, *S/Z*, trans. Richard Miller (New York: Hill and Wang, 1975), 44–45.

16. *Rope*'s aesthetic would thus be fully in keeping with this perennial fashion diktat: "to look right, things should always look ever so slightly wrong." Nick Sullivan, "The Summer Upgrade," *Esquire* 155, nos. 6–7 (June/July 2011): 79.

17. Compare the succession of opening doors in *Spellbound* or the multiple prison entryways in *The Paradine Case*, where the cinematic pun is absent.

18. Though the hidden caricature is unmistakable once you know it's there, in no format of *Rope* have I been able to read the word "Reduco": the blur is irresolvable. Yet Hitchcock himself attests to the word's being there: "The Hitchcock countenance . . . appear[s] in a neon 'Reduco' sign." Alfred Hitchcock, *Hitchcock on Hitchcock: Selected Writings and Interviews*, ed. Sidney Gottlieb (Berkeley: University of California Press, 1995), 282. "Reduco" would

thus be the limit-case of a hidden picture: a thing so well hidden that, without ceasing to exist, it has become *invisible*.

19. Garrett Stewart, *Novel Violence: A Narratography of Victorian Fiction* (Chicago: University of Chicago, 2009).

THE LONG *WRONG MAN*

1. Eve is said to do this to Roger in *North by Northwest*. See also Guy's remark in *Strangers on a Train* that Detective Hennessy "sticks so close that he's beginning to grow on me—like a fungus."

2. "A short story is rarely put down in the middle, and in this sense it resembles a film." Truffaut, *Hitchcock*, 72.

3. See Reuben A. Brower's New Critical essay "Reading in Slow Motion," first published in 1959, and Roland Barthes's narratological claim, in "Textual Analysis of a Tale by Edgar Poe," from 1973, that "this reading will be, as it were, filmed in slow motion." Reuben A. Brower, "Reading in Slow Motion," in *In Defense of Reading: A Reader's Approach to Literary Criticism*, ed. Reuben A. Brower and Richard Poirier (New York: E. P. Dutton, 1962), 3–21; Roland Barthes, "Textual Analysis of a Tale by Edgar Poe," trans. Richard Howard, in *The Semiotic Challenge* (Oxford: Blackwell, 1988), 264. DVD technology allows this practice to be realized, with almost hallucinatory exactitude, in cinema studies.

4. Frederick Foster, "'Hitch' Didn't Want It Arty," *American Cinematographer* (February 1957), 84–85, 112–14.

5. Martin Scorsese on the last episode of Rosselini's *Paisà*, in *My Voyage to Italy* (1999; disc 1, 47:36–39).

6. Marshall Deutelbaum, "Finding the Right Man in *The Wrong Man*," in *The Hitchcock Reader*, ed. Marshall Deutelbaum and Leland Poague, 2nd ed., 212–22 (Oxford: Blackwell, 2009). According to Deutelbaum, the Right Man may be seen not just here but on two other occasions in the film as well:

> As a careful examination of *The Wrong Man* reveals, the real thief is often visible in the film as he and Balestrero cross paths. Balestrero actually bumps into Daniel [the Right Man, played by Robbins] outside the Victor Moore Arcade. . . . After his arrest, the police take Balestrero to a liquor store that had also been robbed to give the employees a chance to identify him. As Manny leaves in a squad-car

afterwards, Daniel walks past the liquor store on the sidewalk. Similarly, after Balestrero is led from a paddy wagon into Felony Court for his arraignment, the camera holds on the scene long enough to show Daniel strolling through the frame after Manny has disappeared from sight. Thus while Daniel's overt appearance late in the film, in the long lap dissolve which superimposes his face on Balestrero's, is generally regarded as the film's most striking device, the dissolve simply makes his presence manifest. (220)

It should be noted Deutelbaum is also jumping the gun in these other cases, which are, to this Too-Close Viewer's eyes, undecidable.

And yet, how congenial I find this account! It is well-attuned to the Hitchcockian game of hidden pictures, of which the critic claims, however erroneously, to have found no fewer than three; and, more generally, it acknowledges the two boards—one for manifest, the other for secret signification—that playing this game requires. I might almost think that, from the mirroring of our initials on, I had found a critical double, and one who, like the Lookalike in relation to Manny, has already been where I am proposing to go.

7. Krohn, *Hitchcock at Work*, 180.

8. E.g., the man in black, having crossed paths with the woman, and the Lookalike, having crossed paths with Manny, then cross one another. Later on (1:00:32–38), when Manny enters the Arcade with Rose, this time to go to O'Connor's office, the pair crosses a male-female couple leaving. Then, in the following dissolve to Manny and Rose in the office corridor, the overlap juxtaposes the vestigial image of Manny, screen right, walking away from us, to the emerging image of Manny, screen left, walking toward us—so that the pattern seems to be repeating with Manny as his *own* double. And finally, Manny has been followed into the arcade by yet another tall man in fedora and overcoat, whose ghost-image in the dissolve quickly replaces Manny's own.

9. I explain. *The Wrong Man* tells a nightmarish tale, but, from a moral standpoint, this grim film is as glib as they come. Most of us watch it in the full conviction that *we* would never make the egregious errors of Manny's accusers; and in this, we are perfectly right: the film is structured so that we never *could* make them. Thanks to the combined labors of *Life* magazine, which first brought Manny

Balestrero's ordeal to general attention, and Warner Bros., invested in getting still wider publicity for its film, we are not only familiar with the story; we are familiar with it *as true*. And were there any doubt of Manny's innocence, the fact that his part is given to Henry Fonda, who (at least until *Once Upon a Time in the West* [1968]) never played a genuinely bad character onscreen, would suffice to dispel it. Prevented by our epistemological advantage from passing a wrong judgment, we all the more smugly attach our opprobrium to the characters who do: the secretaries, the police officers, the prosecutor, even Rose herself (whose insanity is most convincingly rendered in this one symptom: she doubts Manny). The eyes of all seem to us as obviously blinded by likeness or likelihood as our own are fixed throughout on nothing but the truth.

"I think the man at the window is the one that's been here before." These are the words of a secretary at Associated Life; but, in the kind of error she makes, she might as well be Deutelbaum telling us that the man we see in the dissolve is the one we earlier saw "actually bump into" Manny in the Arcade. If this hapless critic were an onscreen character, we would group him with Manny's accusers, who likewise affirm an identity where none exists. But if these accusers were watching the film instead of appearing in it, what kind of spectators would they be? They would not resemble, certainly, the Too-Close Viewer. They would have little talent for recognizing continuity errors, and even less inclination to develop one. They would be too preoccupied with inserting the film into the déjà vu of films, novels, and myths known beforehand; and too busy acquiescing in the naturalness of a spectacle where everything, from character to story to enunciation to style, is supposed to hold together, and where their own role as spectators is only to bear witness to this coherence. Curiously, in other words, while a demonstrably wrongheaded spectator like Deutelbaum would readily join the cast of wrongheaded characters, these same unworthy beings, once they were transformed into spectators, would become perfectly exemplary. They would become the very public that classic Hollywood cinema, with its abundant continuity rules for film form, and its endless recirculation of stereotypes in film content, does everything to encourage and reward.

Insofar, then, as we *are* these "good" spectators (and in the the-

ater, it is hard to be otherwise), our conviction that Manny is innocent replicates the closure of the "bad" characters' assumption
that he is not. We secure our certitude by resorting to the previously
known (*Life* magazine) or the elsewhere seen (Henry Fonda in *The
Grapes of Wrath* [1940]), just as the police and prosecutor build their
case against Manny on its congruence to an old crime novel (playing
the horses, working in a nightclub, money troubles with the mob—
"it all adds up"). And no more than the secretaries are we open to
doubting our opinion, or to allowing the labor of looking to mediate
between our impression and our judgment, which are born in the
same instant. As a rule, of course, we are perfectly unaware that our
being in the right is homologous to *their* being in the wrong; the
mirroring of mentalities occurs across levels of discourse—film
narrative and film watching—which classic cinema rarely brings
into direct contact. Thus, in our blinded eyes as "good" spectators,
close attention is an obvious virtue that certain characters in the
story would have done well to cultivate, but it is never a virtue required by our own viewing practice, in which to tell Henry Fonda
from the others is the easiest thing in the world.

10. Even in this instance, such an ethics is not *sure*. After all, it is
just possible that Hitchcock, meaning to do precisely what Deutelbaum sees him as having done, let a different actor play the Right
Man in the Arcade scene, in the belief that a theatrically captive
audience, even seeing the film more than once, wouldn't be able to
remember the details of an anonymous face they saw for a couple
of seconds. In that case, the Too-Close Viewer who pointed out the
difference between the two actors would not be modeling a moral
gesture, but merely observing a continuity error perhaps better left
unnoticed.

11. "This is Alfred Hitchcock speaking. In the past, I have given
you many kinds of suspense pictures; but this time I would like you
to see a different one. The difference lies in the fact that this is a
true story. . . ." Critics tend to locate *The Wrong Man*'s exceptionality
in the difference Hitchcock explicitly states—the difference that
"a true story" is supposed to make—but his words have indicated
another difference before that one is stated. He doesn't quite say
this—from a marketing angle, it would be highly unwise—but it
seems on the tip of his tactful tongue: *The Wrong Man* is not a sus-

pense picture at all. Jean-Luc Godard gets the point right when, in his essay on the film, he wrongly quotes the above remark thus: "This film resembles none of my other films. There is no suspense. Nothing but the truth." Jean-Luc Godard, "*The Wrong Man*," in *Godard on Godard: Critical Writings*, trans. and ed. Tom Milne (New York: Da Capo, 1986), 48. See also François Truffaut, "*The Wrong Man*," in *The Films in My Life*, trans. Leonard Mayhew (New York: Da Capo, 1994), 85.

12. Godard has, memorably, made the same point about *all* of Hitchcock's films: "We have forgotten why Joan Fontaine leans over the edge of a cliff, and what Joel McCrea had gone to do in Holland. We have forgotten why Montgomery Clift remains forever silent and why Janet Leigh stops at the Bates Motel and why Teresa Wright is still in love with Uncle Charlie. We have forgotten what Henry Fonda is not entirely guilty of and why exactly the US government hires Ingrid Bergman. But we remember a handbag. But we remember a bus in the desert. But we remember a glass of milk, the vanes of a windmill, a hairbrush. But we remember a row of bottles, a pair of glasses, a sheet of music, a set of keys" (Jean-Luc Godard, *Histoire(s) du cinéma* [1998; Olive Films, 2011], disc 2, 12:11–13:38). With *The Wrong Man*, however, our sense of plot is defective not simply in retrospect, but even while we are watching the film. The final script did include a scene between O'Connor and his assistant in which we learn that the missing witness, found at last, would corroborate Manny's alibi, but Hitchcock cut the scene—and in the bargain deleted the very mention of an alibi from O'Connor's opening address to the jury.

13. So light is the burden placed on our vision that, occasionally, it doesn't matter whether we even *see* what a sufficiently good authority assures us is visible. Most viewers of *Rear Window* discern no difference when comparing Jefferies's slide of the flower bed to the flower bed itself until Jefferies points this difference out ("since when do flowers grow shorter in two weeks?"); as soon he does, however, the same viewers will swear it exists.

14. Bonitzer, "Hitchcockian Suspense."

15. Recall this example from the previous essay: "We have a very simple excuse [for not serving dinner on the dining room table] right here"—Brandon means the books lying near the cassone; but

in showing us the books, Hitchcock also shows us the fatal rope sticking out of the cassone, which Brandon hasn't seen; and from that position, the camera easily closes in on Brandon's back to mask the cut to the next take. If Brandon's naïve practice of perfectionism is ruined by a series of oversights, Hitchcock's ironic practice of "the necessary mistake" seems, on the contrary, rather perfect: in both senses of the word, he owns (admits, masters) his mistakes.

16. Hitchcock may also have been indulging in a sort of product placement for Bickford's here. There was some worry during production that the Bickford's name would be seen onscreen and create a permissions problem. It seems to have been resolved by treating the cafeteria to free advertisement, highlighting the name and linking it to friendly service: "Shall I bring your toast to the table, Manny?" is an otherwise preposterous question, given that Manny orders this same thing every morning.

Whether owing to more product placement (Bristol-Meyers was the first sponsor of *Alfred Hitchcock Presents*) or Hitchcock's usual fondness for crystalline images, the bottle of Bufferin on Rose's bedside table gets the same treatment as the Bickford's cup; when the angle changes, the bottle is rotated so that we still see the label from the front.

17. Not only do numbers abound in Hitchcock's cinema as in no other; they have an obsessional distinctness. Note how, earlier in *The Wrong Man*, the address numbers on Manny's doorstep—numbers he will be obliged to repeat many times—gleam under the night lights. As this example shows, while Hitchcock's numbers are always fully legible, the reasons for their legibility are not always easily statable. Present a strong visual emphasis, but absent any comparably strong narrative justification for it, his numerals seem numerological, harboring some secret significance if only we could crack the code. And, at least in a broad sense, we can. Unlucky thirteen, of course, obtrudes all over the place, either in itself (as in the Lodger's address or on the church clock whose hands forever tell 1:30 in *Murder!* [1934]); in its multiples (Eve Kendall is twenty-six, there are thirty-nine steps); or as the sum of another number's digits: Marion Crane's license plates jinx the newly purchased car she drives to the Bates Motel, and even before Stella "smells trouble" in *Rear Window*, we've *seen* it indicated by the mercury level on Jefferies's thermom-

eter, which has climbed to an admonitory 94 degrees. Even apart from this tireless mining of triskaidekaphobia, the mere fact of number, of any number at all, is ominous in Hitchcock. So strict is his rule that there be no number without impending danger, and no danger without an attendant number, that he is even compelled to enumerate the middle of nowhere: "Prairie Stop, Highway 41."

Sooner or later, *every* number in Hitchcock becomes an unlucky thirteen, the confirmed address or time of an appointment with the Hitchcockian Thing. But here it is Hitchcock, rather than his protagonist, who keeps that appointment. The fateful determination of Number, in addition to spelling bad luck *in* the movie, spells a bit of bad luck *for* the movie, which has momentarily fallen victim to its own numerological hexing.

18. The error notwithstanding, the shot is another instance of Hitchcock's sly fondness for literalizing cinematic devices—the tracking shot of train tracks in *Strangers*, the framing of hall and door frames in *Rope*, the cuts on knife-cuts in *Psycho*, etc.

19. Charades abound throughout Hitchcock's oeuvre. The climax of *Saboteur* (1942) seems to exist mainly for the sake of literalizing the expression "his life is hanging by a thread"; and, just as *Lifeboat* (1944) never stops insisting that its characters are "all in the same boat," so even *Psycho* is arguably little more than an elaborate ruse to introduce the jokey image of a Mother who, whatever irreparable damage she may have done, literally "wouldn't harm a fly." Even *The Wrong Man*, whose serious-mindedness should offer no occasion for playing charades, has its share of them. In the classic manner of Hitchcock's psychotics, Rose enacts her insanity as the literalization of a figure of speech. "They'll smash us!" she says and, making a charade of her own words, promptly smashes Manny's head with her hairbrush. A more strenuous riddle is presented in the "a bit too self-evident" continuity error that occurs when the police, searching for more crimes to pin on Manny, make him walk in and out of a recently robbed liquor store. A placard that reads "by the case" hangs just above him as he enters the store (24:13–15), and, unaccountably, it jumps to the opposite wall so as to remain above him, like a supertitle, when he leaves it (24:47–51). With this signage, Hitchcock is doubtless referencing Manny Balestrero's own "case" (the *Life* magazine source article for the film was called "A Case of Identity"); and by means of the faulty

continuity, he is bringing the factitiousness of such apparent open-and-shut cases to bear on our normal viewing practice.

20. Renata Salecl, in a provocative account of *The Wrong Man* that I consider more fully in note 22, would dispute this claim. About the late confrontation between Manny and Rose in their bedroom, she writes, "Rose stops in front of the mirror . . ." and illustrates this action with an image in which, indisputably, Rose does stand fully reflected in the bedroom mirror. I can only invite my readers to verify with their own eyes that *no such image exists in Hitchcock's film*; I suspect it is a production still. Renata Salecl, "The Right Man and the Wrong Woman," in Žižek, *Everything You Always Wanted to Know*, 191.

21. In her admirably close account of the deformation of Manny's face, Noa Steimatsky observes that the crucial first misidentification of Manny (by a clerk at Associated Life) involves framing his face in relation to a *grid*; such framings, she shows, become the norm during the course of Manny's indictment. In contrast to the "honorific" close-ups of Manny at the beginning of the film, these barred images offer evidence of "the subjugation of the individual to social and institutional scrutiny" and, more particularly, to the criminalizing anthropometric measures pioneered by Lombroso, Galton, and Bertillon in the nineteenth century. For Steimatsky, Hitchcock's own film is complicit in this anthropometric scrutiny of its protagonist; we participate in the clerk's reading, she writes, "even as we know it to be false." Here, though, I'd reverse her emphasis; when Hitchcock makes us see what the clerk sees (or when later, at the trial, he makes us see what another clerk sees), he is employing a "free indirect vision" that rehearses the culpabilizing perspective ironically, letting us recognize it as such. See Noa Steimatsky, "What the Clerk Saw: Face to Face with *The Wrong Man*," *Framework* 48, no. 2 (Fall 2007): 111–36.

22. Salecl's argument is that "Rose's psychosis is ultimately a reflection of Manny's: by taking the guilt upon herself and going mad, she makes it possible for Manny to preserve his attitude of psychotic indifference—since she takes the role of the wrong woman, of a being burdened with guilt, he is able to keep on living as the right man freed from guilt. Since she assumes the role of a 'public' madwoman, *his madness* can continue to wear the public mask of normality." Salecl,

"Right Man," 193. Rose does appear to "catch" the derangement her husband is repressing, in the same transferential pattern that makes her suffer the toothache he got over the month before; but it is disingenuous to regard Manny as a successful male paragon of normality, particularly when Salecl is often merely translating into Lacanese the common irritation with his gutlessness. After all, Manny, too, is shown to be paying a price for the Other's normality: his "psychotic indifference" is, among other things, a response to a carceral system that produces delinquents on whom to project its own crazy-making incoherence. A neat example of this projection occurs at the police station when, writing down the holdup man's note being dictated to him, Manny misspells "drawer" as "draw." As this happens to have been the holdup man's error, too, the police regard it as a virtual confession. But the error Manny has unconsciously reproduced is not that of the thief who wrote the note but that of the detective who has just read it out, and whom we have distinctly heard say, betraying an ethnic history of his own, "draw," not "drawer."

In this context, it is worth reconsidering the weird circle shot of Manny in his cell—weird because, though it seems to be representing Manny's own dizziness, it is distinctly *not* Manny's point of view. I have suggested that, in an act of supreme identification, Hitchcock's camera is performing Manny's own vertigo *for him*. But something else is implied as well: that Manny's vertigo is being projected upon him by a "system" that lies outside him. Hitchcock's camera would thus be simultaneously identified not just with Manny, but with the carceral institution that spins him in this vicious circle. Against Salecl's account of Rose, I'd similarly argue that Rose is not just sacrificially allowing Manny to wear the mask of sanity, but also, more aggressively, attempting to mar that mask so that Manny can never be, feel, or even seem normal again. And she has a certain measure of success; after the mistrial, Manny, sounding just like Rose, says to his mother: "I brought it all on myself. . . . I've been such an idiot that you'd all be better off without me."

23. "When I was six months old," Hitchcock was fond of recalling, "I was in my mother's arms, and she went 'Boo!' and scared the hell out of me and gave me the hiccups." If Manny's incarceration repeats Hitchcock's remembered childhood experience in prison, where his father sent him to be punished, and so generated his "eter-

nal fear of the police," Rose's hairbrush reenacts the equally primal maternal startlement whose rhythm Hitchcock's cinema rehearses too obsessively to suggest that he ever got over those hiccups. See Truffaut, *Hitchcock*, 205. The Mother and the Police: Hitchcock's two greatest themes, two greatest fears, two greatest inspirations for the disconcerting ruptures of his "little touches."

24. Salecl, who also notices that the mirror-shot cannot be Manny's point of view, argues "that the only standpoint where the gaze could come from is *the standpoint of the table lamp.*" Salecl, "Right Man," 191–92. We needn't bother wondering which table lamp she is referring to—there are two of them in the scene—since we have occasion to see Manny towering over each; the standpoint of either would give us a noticeably lower angle than the one from which the image has been taken.

25. Slavoj Žižek, "'In His Bold Gaze My Ruin Is Writ Large,'" in Žižek, *Everything You Always Wanted to Know*, 216. Žižek makes the same argument in an earlier essay, "*Le faux coupable:* L'échec du métalanguage" (*The Wrong Man:* The Failure of Metalanguage) which appeared in a similarly titled, but entirely different, French collection, *Tout ce que vous avez toujours voulu savoir sur Lacan sans jamais oser le demander à Hitchcock*, ed. Slavoj Žižek (Marsat, France: Navarin, 1988), 161–64. Neither account suggests that this brilliant popularizer of Lacan has paid much attention to *The Wrong Man*. In the 1988 essay, he tells us that Manny "is arrested for murders he didn't commit" (161); and when this information is corrected in the 1992 essay, it remains erroneous: Manny is now said to be arrested for a bank robbery. Let me add that, in his work on Hitchcock in general, Žižek makes so many errors, visual as well as narrative, that they seem nothing short of programmatic. In order to get his totalizing Lacanian allegory, he evidently shrinks from interrogating the actual films and relies instead on received notions that circulate around them. It is as though he actually *were* "afraid to ask" Hitchcock about Lacan, lest the artist prove as difficult as the thinker he is supposed to make easy.

26. And not just musically: convulsively developed, the motif cues the enigmatic circle shot in which the camera orbits irregularly around Manny's face, seeming to enact *Hitchcock's* dizzy spell rather than represent Manny's.

27. The silhouette obviously alludes to the introduction to the *Alfred Hitchcock Presents* television series; but here, Hitchcock faces us head on, so that his features and girth, unmistakably specific when seen from the side, are obscured. And while, on TV, Hitchcock reappears after the silhouette to address the audience face to face under proper studio lighting, here the frontal silhouette remains his *only* mode of self-presentation. I note by the way that in one episode Hitchcock refers to the double modality of his TV appearance as "me and my shadow" ("John Brown's Body," December 30, 1956), but it seems that even in the series the shadow is felt to have ontological priority: "I'm as real as a piece of motion picture film, as authentic as a shadow" ("And The Desert Shall Bloom," December 21, 1958).

28. William Rothman, *Must We Kill the Thing We Love? Emersonian Perfectionism and the Films of Alfred Hitchcock* (New York: Columbia University Press, 2014), 188.

29. The same question—is Hitchcock whoever says he is?—is posed in comic terms in "The Case of Mr. Pelham," an 1955 episode of *Alfred Hitchcock Presents* that Hitchcock directed at the same time he was working on *The Wrong Man*. In the story proper, Mr. Albert Pelham is stalked by a lookalike who finally succeeds in driving him crazy. "He's been put away," says the lookalike, now established as the real Mr. Pelham. "I don't think he'll ever be right again." In Hitchcock's customary coda to the story, we see men in white coats attempting to put *him* away, too. "But I'm Alfred Hitchcock!" he protests. "I am! I can prove it!" To which one of the men wisecracks: "Sure, sure, everybody is." And no sooner is Hitchcock strongarmed out of sight than the camera pans in the opposite direction to reveal . . . another Hitchcock, who, concerned but unruffled, has been observing the whole unfortunate business from the wings. This second Hitchcock comments on the first: "An astounding hoax; he carried off the impersonation brilliantly." Such self-doubling recurs throughout Hitchcock's TV appearances.

30. A first, "classic" answer: it is true to the traditional narrative structure in which the beginning will be matched up with the end. In addition to this prologue, *The Wrong Man* has framed the drama proper with an equally solemn and overstated epilogue. A closing title alleges that Rose, whose eyes we have last seen glazed over in psychotic withdrawal, would later be "completely cured"; "today she

lives happily in Florida with Manny and the two boys. . . ." And just as the doubtful opening image of Hitchcock belies the transparency of his words, so the even more doubtful closing image of Manny, Rose, and the two boys, walking along Biscayne Boulevard in Miami, contradicts the cheering title. We see the figures only from behind, in a wide shot; tiny to begin with, they walk away from us into what (considering the direction of the shadows cast by the palm trees) is certainly not the sunset. The boys are appropriately wearing Bermudas, but Manny, in his iconic dark suit and fedora, remains dressed for a New York January. Given the wide shot, of course, there would otherwise be no way of identifying him as Manny. And we are given that wide shot, also of course, because he is *not* Manny—not at least the Manny who looks exactly like Henry Fonda, but only so inadequate a lookalike that the camera dare not get closer. In the very shot meant to confirm that Manny and Rose have regained happiness, we can't tell that it *is* Manny and Rose; indeed, we are pretty certain it is not. The wrong-man problematic latent in the introductory image returns in the final one even as the title seeks to lay it to rest. Seldom has the lie of the Hollywood ending been told so unconvincingly.

31. Dan Auiler, *Hitchcock's Notebooks* (New York: Avon, 1999), 474. I have reproduced not Auiler's nonchalantly cropped image, but the integral photograph from the Warner Bros. Archive.

32. I think of the gorgeous production still from *Notorious* (1946), reproduced in the front matter of Krohn, *Hitchcock at Work*, in which Hitchcock is shown putting a packet of poison into a cup of coffee while Ingrid Bergman, already holding a coffee cup in hand, looks on in understandable confusion.

33. Mrs. Danvers occupies this position while prodding the heroine of *Rebecca* (1940) to commit suicide; so does Keller when tormenting Father Logan during the great tracking sequence in *I Confess* (1952). And more mundanely, at the start of *Dial M for Murder*, Tony Wendice throws spilt table salt over his left shoulder.

34. Hitchcock expounds this amazing effect in discussing *Rear Window* with Truffaut:

[In Kuleshov's experiment] you see a close-up of the Russian actor Ivan Mosjoukine. This is immediately followed by a shot of a dead baby. Back to Mosjoukine again and you read compassion on his face. Then you take away the dead baby and you show a bowl of soup, and now, when you go back to Mosjoukine, he looks hungry. Yet, in both cases, they used the same shot of the actor; his face was exactly the same.

In the same way, let's take a close up of [James] Stewart looking out of the window at a little dog that's being lowered in a basket. Back to Stewart who has a kindly smile. But in the place of the little dog you show a half-naked girl exercising in front of her open window, and you go back to a smiling Stewart again, this time he's seen as a dirty old man. (Truffaut, *Hitchcock*, 214–16)

But where Kuleshov's experiment seems to be making a general point about perception by association, Hitchcock's iteration harnesses the effect to the more specific work of producing "the stain": a sudden saturation of the ordinary and benign by the sinister and guilt-laden. He rebrands the effect even more plainly in a 1964 TV interview for which he refilms the experiment with his own person replacing Stewart's as the initially good-hearted but ultimately "dirty" old man. (https://www.youtube.com/watch?v=hCAEot6KwJY).

35. In his classic analysis of Melanie's motorboat ride in *The Birds*, Raymond Bellour observes a comparable moment. See Raymond Bellour, "System of a Fragment (on *The Birds*)," trans. Ben Brewster, in *The Analysis of Film*, ed. Constance Penley, (Bloomington: Indiana University Press, 2000), 28–67. Dominating her outbound trip to Mitch's house is an alternation of images of "Melanie seeing" with images of "what Melanie sees." But on her return to town, thanks to the binoculars we see Mitch turn on her, the familiar image of "Melanie seeing" suddenly becomes an image of "Melanie seen." The function of such theatrical reciprocity, Bellour argues, "is to carry to its highest pitch the binary action seeing/seen governed by the principle of alternation, that is, to effect its reversal into seeing/seeing" (52–53). The dual seeing opens up a "murderous relationship" (63) between Mitch and Melanie, in which the female partner quickly comes to bear the brunt of its mutual, but inequitably distributed, aggression. In *The Wrong Man*, it is the man who, already diminished as "Manny," falls victim to the hetero-ocular exchange.

36. This flickering—uneven, unpredictable, jagged—gives the cameo a visual rhythm that the continuous appearances lack. If we could *hear* such a rhythm in Hitchcock—and of course we do, often—it would sound like the rattle of the fire extinguisher in the truck cab in *Saboteur*, the clip-clop of footsteps following Ben Mc-Kenna on his way to meet Ambrose Chappell in *The Man Who Knew Too Much*, the tap-tapping on the window in *Marnie* (1964), Brandon's stammer in *Rope*, the morbid twittering in *The Birds*, or the shattering of glass in almost *every* Hitchcock film. It's a common visual rhythm in the oeuvre, too; we experience it in the twitching of the drummer's eye in *Young and Innocent* (1937), the fireworks display in *To Catch a Thief* (1955), and the tremor of Alicia's hand during the key-shot of *Notorious*. It is often enacted by the camera as a quick series of jump cuts: when Bruno is jostled into dropping Guy's lighter down a sewer; when Daisy's father falls in *The Lodger* (1926); when Jack Favell surprises the second Mrs. De Winter from behind in *Rebecca*; when the pecans spill on the floor in *Marnie*; and practically anywhere in *Psycho* or *The Birds*, which together represent Hitchcock's stylistic coming-out, when this rhythm enters into its own.

This irregular succession of little jolts is a far cry from the legato or "bound" rhythm of suspense, where a clock is typically on hand to measure and give efficient organization to what we see onscreen. But neither can it be thought of as the rhythm of surprise, which Hitchcock often proposes as suspense's inferior opposite. As a single, nonrepeated event, surprise has no rhythm at all; to take Hitchcock's own mimetically curt example, "Boom! There is an explosion." The true opposite of Hitchcockian suspense is not singular surprise, but frequentative startlement. More: this startlement provides the stimulus to the very formation of suspense, whose essentially reactive function is to unify an otherwise overwhelming spate of agitations under a glazelike smoothness of vision. Hitchcock is the Master of Suspense only insofar as suspense is the master of startlement. (The greatness of his achievement may be indicated by a fact familiar to anyone who has quit smoking: a single "craving" lasts a mere three seconds, but cravings come every *two* seconds.) And still more: startlement, as Hitchcock lets us understand it, may be the fundamental rhythm of cinema itself, with its radical, if usually invisible, discontinuity between images; and if it is, Hitchcock's cinema would also let us understand why cinema, in its most intense examples, is unbearably hard to watch.

I discern three interrelated levels at which startlement is experienced in Hitchcock. First, startlement may take the form of an actual event in the world. The extinguisher's rattle, for instance, is said by the truck driver to "get to you"; and, about the tap-tapping in *Marnie*, the heroine says that "it means they want in." Second, such startlement being intrinsically infectious, this event has the power to produce, in the very defense against it, a mimetic startlement emanating from the character. Not so much deeply internalized as superficially mirrored, startlement becomes the personality-structure of the "nervous" character. Thus, Marnie, even in repressing the tapping, has always-already assimilated it as her own repulsive jumpiness. And the many other high-strung characters are not so lucky as she to find the therapeutic "key" to their skittishness in a buried trauma. If Bruno's abrupt mood swings, like Norman's, die with him, the unnerving nervousness of Emma Newton in *Shadow of a Doubt* (1943), or Lina in *Suspicion* (1941), promises to be interminable. And third, the same infectious spirit enters the spectator, who typically contracts startlement from event and character alike. If, in a state of suspense, we are what is commonly called a bundle of nerves, under the worse condition of startlement, it is as if these nerves have been *un*bundled and their impulses were firing disconnectedly and at random.

37. But isn't this what you see if you look long and close enough at *anything*? Not necessarily. Looking long and intensely might just as easily secure an impression of unity; a case in point is the trance-like monotony induced by the recurring Manny Shot, which serves to mask Hitchcock's sudden discontinuous appearance. As the hidden transference and the hidden cameo both go to show, *The Wrong Man* is actively, if secretly, espousing a Heraclitean vision in which no man steps into the same river twice. It is doing so, I've suggested, not only to put forward a philosophy of being, or a theory of cinema-as-discontinuity, but also, through these means, as a counteraction of the sting of misrecognition suffered by both its protagonist and its director. The personal predicament of being misrecognized is universalized as a world in which *everything* must be misrecognized.

Bibliography

The first book on Hitchcock as an esoteric artist is Jean Douchet's *Alfred Hitchcock* (Paris: Editions de l'Herne, 1967). It is nowhere cited but everywhere presupposed in these pages.

Allen, Richard. *Hitchcock's Romantic Irony*. New York: Columbia University Press, 2007.

Auiler, Dan. *Hitchcock's Notebooks*. New York: Avon, 1999.

Barthes, Roland. *Mythologies*. Translated by Annette Lavers. New York: Hill and Wang, 1972.

———. *S/Z*. Translated by Richard Miller. New York: Hill and Wang, 1975.

———. "Textual Analysis of a Tale by Edgar Poe." Translated by Richard Howard. In *The Semiotic Challenge*, 261–93. Oxford: Blackwell, 1988.

Barton, Sabrina. "'Crisscross': Paranoia and Projection in *Strangers on a Train*." In *Out in Culture: Gay, Lesbian and Queer Essays on Popular Culture*, edited by Corey K. Creekmur and Alexander Doty, 216–38. Durham, NC: Duke University Press, 1995.

Bellour, Raymond. *The Analysis of Film*. Edited by Constance Penley. Bloomington: Indiana University Press, 2000.

———. "Symbolic Blockage." Translated by Mary Quaintance. In Bellour, *Analysis of Film*, 77–192.

———. "System of a Fragment (on *The Birds*)." Translated by Ben Brewster. In Bellour, *Analysis of Film*, 28–67.

Best, Stephen, and Sharon Marcus. "Surface Reading: An Introduction." *Representations*, no. 108 (2009), 1–21.

Bonitzer, Pascal. "Hitchcockian Suspense." Translated by Martin Thom. In Žižek, *Everything You Always Wanted to Know about Lacan (But Were Afraid to Ask Hitchcock)*, 15–30.

Booth, Stephen. *Precious Nonsense*. Berkeley: University of California Press, 1998.

Bordwell, David. *Poetics of Cinema*. New York: Routledge, 2008.

Brower, Reuben A. "Reading in Slow Motion." In *In Defense of Reading: A Reader's Approach to Literary Criticism*, edited by Reuben A. Brower and Richard Poirier, 3–21. New York: E. P. Dutton, 1962.

Clark, T. J. *The Sight of Death*. New Haven, CT: Yale University Press, 2006.

Cohen, Tom. *Hitchcock's Cryptonymies*. 2 vols. Minneapolis: University of Minnesota Press, 2005.

Deutelbaum, Marshall. "Finding the Right Man in *The Wrong Man*." In *The Hitchcock Reader*, edited by Marshall Deutelbaum and Leland Poague, 2nd ed., 212–22. Oxford: Blackwell, 2009.

Edelman, Lee. *No Future*. Durham, NC: Duke University Press, 2004.

Fisher, Philip. *The Vehement Passions*. Princeton, NJ: Princeton University Press, 2003.

Foster, Frederick. "'Hitch' Didn't Want It Arty." *American Cinematographer* (February 1957), 84–85, 112–14.

Godard, Jean-Luc. "*The Wrong Man*." In *Godard on Godard: Critical Writings*. Translated and edited by Tom Milne, 48–55. New York: Da Capo, 1986.

Hitchcock, Alfred. *Hitchcock on Hitchcock: Selected Writings and Interviews*. Edited by Sidney Gottlieb. Berkeley: University of California Press, 1995.

Krohn, Bill. *Hitchcock at Work*. London: Phaidon, 2000.

Leitch, Thomas M. *Find the Director and Other Hitchcock Games*. Athens, GA: University of Georgia Press, 1991.

Mather, Philippe. "Shot Transitions and Narrative Logic in Hitchcock's *Rope*." *Kinema* (Spring 2009). http://www.kinema.uwaterloo.ca/article.php?id=446&feature.

Miller, D. A. "Anal *Rope*." *Representations*, no. 32 (1990), 114–33.

Moretti, Franco. *Distant Reading*. London: Verso, 2013.

Mulvey, Laura. *Death 24x a Second: Stillness and the Moving Image*. London: Reaktion, 2006.

Perkins, V. F. "*Rope.*" *Movie* 7 (1963): 11–13.

Rohmer, Eric. "Roberto Rossellini: *Stromboli.*" In *The Taste for Beauty*. Translated by Carol Volk, 124–27. Cambridge: Cambridge University Press, 1989. Originally published in *La gazette du cinéma* 5 (November 1950).

Rohmer, Eric, and Claude Chabrol. *Hitchcock: The First Forty-Four Films*. Translated by Stanley Hochman. New York: Continuum, 1988.

Rope. New York: Dell, 1948.

Rothman, William. *The Murderous Gaze*. 2nd ed. Albany: State University of New York Press, 2012.

———. *Must We Kill the Thing We Love? Emersonian Perfectionism and the Films of Alfred Hitchcock*. New York: Columbia University Press, 2014.

Salecl, Renata. "The Right Man and the Wrong Woman." In Žižek, *Everything You Always Wanted to Know about Lacan (But Were Afraid to Ask Hitchcock)*.

Sarris, Andrew. "Hitchcock." In *Focus on Hitchcock*, edited by Albert J. LaValley, 87–90. Englewood Cliffs, NJ: Prentice-Hall,1972.

Spoto, Donald. *The Dark Side of Genius*. New York: Ballantine, 1983.

Steimatsky, Noa. "What the Clerk Saw: Face to Face with *The Wrong Man*." *Framework* 48, no. 2 (Fall 2007): 111–36.

Stewart, Garrett. *Novel Violence: A Narratography of Victorian Fiction*. Chicago: University of Chicago Press, 2009.

Sullivan, Nick. "The Summer Upgrade." *Esquire* 155, nos. 6–7 (June/July 2011): 79.

Truffaut, François. "A Certain Tendency of the French Cinema." In *Movies and Methods: An Anthology*, vol. 1, edited by Bill Nichols, 224–37. Berkeley: University of California Press, 1976. Originally published as "Une certaine tendance du cinéma français," *Cahiers du cinéma* 31 (1964).

———. *Hitchcock*. With Helen G. Scott. New York: Simon & Schuster, 1984.

———. "*The Wrong Man*." In *The Films in My Life*. Translated by Leonard Mayhew, 83–86. New York: Da Capo, 1994.

Žižek, Slavoj. *Everything You Always Wanted to Know About Lacan (But Were Afraid to Ask Hitchcock)*. London: Verso, 1992.

———. "Le faux coupable: L'échec du métalanguage." In *Tout ce que vous avez toujours voulu savoir sur Lacan sans jamais oser le demander à Hitchcock*, edited by Slavoj Žižek, 161–64. Marsat, France: Navarin, 1988.

———. "'In His Bold Gaze My Ruin Is Writ Large.'" In Žižek, *Everything You Always Wanted to Know about Lacan (But Were Afraid to Ask Hitchcock)*, 211–72.

Milton Keynes UK
Ingram Content Group UK Ltd.
UKHW020053091223
434043UK00014B/717

9 780226 514345